When the Grain Ran True

Memoirs of a Major League Bat Boy

By Glenn R. Davis

Andrew Benzie Books
Orinda, California

Published by Andrew Benzie Books
www.andrewbenziebooks.com

Comments? grdavis2011@gmail.com

Printed in the United States of America

First Edition: April 2015

10 9 8 7 6 5 4 3 2 1

ISBN 978-1-941713-02-0

Cover and book design by Andrew Benzie

The greatest gift a man can receive is to be blessed with good children.
God went way beyond that for me when He brought two such amazing
people into the world in you, my son and daughter.

From the first day my fingers touched the keyboard, this book was written
with both of you in the forefront of my mind. Thanks for being the wonderful
people you have become and for all the joy you have brought into my life.

It is with great pride that I dedicate this Memoir to
you my beloved children, Chris and Ashley.
The grain has always run true in each of you.

With all my love,
Dad

TABLE OF CONTENTS

THE GAME

Nineteen Hundred Sixty-Five. Fifty years ago, and sometimes it still seems like yesterday. This Game has a way of doing that. Whether you are a player, a manager, a coach, a fan, a fry cook at a ballpark concession stand or one of the other members of the cast of characters that make *the* Game special, it stays with you.

A News Highlight Reel from 1965 could have read as follows:

As the nation still mourns the loss of President Kennedy, President Johnson outlines his vision for the "Great Society"... The Vietnam War now rages with over 150,000 additional U.S. troops deployed... The New York Jets sign Joe Namath to Quarterback their team... Martin Luther King marches from Selma to Montgomery, AL and the Voting Rights Act is enacted... The Beatles continue to top the music chart... A routine traffic stop in Los Angeles spurs the Watts Riots... The Sound of Music, Mary Poppins and Goldfinger captivate moviegoers... Health warnings now adorn cigarette packs...The Houston Astrodome opens and Mickey Mantle hits the first indoor home run in baseball history... Muhammad Ali KO's Sonny Liston in a controversial Heavyweight Title rematch... Yankee pitcher Mel Stottlemyre hits an inside-the-park grand slam... Bert "Campy" Campaneris of the Kansas City Athletics becomes the first player in history to play all nine positions in one Major League game, even pitching ambidextrously in his one inning of work on the mound... Ford introduces the Mustang Fastback... Steve McQueen becomes Nevada Smith... and much, much more. 1965 was quite a year!

The absolute disillusionment caused by the assassination of a beloved president, the escalation of war in Southeast Asia, the changing values and roles within the American family and the increasing tensions as many fought for their civil rights, all weighed heavily on our nation. Baseball was impacted by the times as many players were subject to the military draft... many were lost forever.

And through all of that, baseball endured, flourished and even evolved in 1965. Yes, these epic events happened over fifty years ago in my life. But, there was more, much more. For me, 1965 was to become *My Year*. This is my story of that glorious year, and beyond. So please enjoy my Memoirs, from *Then and Now*.

*   *   *

It was an era before steroids and human growth hormones. From what I witnessed, beer, aspirin and tobacco seemed to be the main performance enhancers in those days! There was no free-agency... the owners were mostly that, **owners** and only stardom gave a player any real kind of leverage at all with many of them. The "Reserve Clause" in each player's contract bound them to their respective team in perpetuity, unless ownership decided otherwise.

It was a time before corked bats exploded in the hands of pretenders, before hundred million dollar player contracts and shortly after the retirement of many of the immortals of the game like Gehrig, Ruth, DiMaggio and the like. In this emerging time zone of history, baseball fought to secure its place in a rapidly transitioning world. New stars had risen and more were on their way. However, the coming years would hold many challenges for baseball and our country.

Gehrig and Ruth

It was a time when it no longer much mattered where you came from or what you looked like. Sure, racial issues still existed just as they do today. But, *if you could play*, you could play; even in the "Big Leagues." Jackie Robinson, Larry Doby, Roberto Clemente, and Juan Marichal and the like had already seen to that. It was truly the beginning of an era when a young ball player from a barrio, a ghetto or even a remote cornfield in Iowa could each earn their way to play in Major League's All-Star Classic… if they were good enough… and many were.

Yes, baseball learned somewhat before other parts of our culture that folks from all walks of life cared more about performance on the field, than race or religion off it… after all, it was about the GAME.

It was a time when many fans still "dressed" to go cheer on their favorite team.

*Fans Came Dressed to Win at Comiskey Park,
AKA White Sox Park, in Those Days.*

As a side note, the names Comiskey Park and White Sox Park were used fairly interchangeably during those days as ownership worked to update the image of the old ball yard. You will probably see me doing the same here-in.

There was a certain pride and formality that still existed at a ballpark in 1965. The ushers all wore blue, military style wool suits with brimmed, officer-style hats to do their work... and they were always kind enough to escort you to your seat if you so wished. My brother Larry served as one of those fellows at White Sox Park during that summer.

Andy Frain Usher Helps a Fan With Their Tickets at Comiskey.

There were no cell phones to distract, no video games to emulate. No, this was still a time when the sights, smells, tastes, sounds and excitement of being at the ballpark were all-consuming and often priceless. Barely a game went by when history was not made in some way and the fans were a big part of that experience. They focused on each blazing fastball, on each crack of the bat and on each of the lightning-fast plays made on the field. Often they would be rewarded with something special.

Hall of Famer Sandy Koufax Pitched a Perfect Game in 1965.

There were no instant replays to watch, so the intensity each fan brought to their seats was often fever-pitched. But win or lose, they always got their money's worth. Sure, once in a while a heated discussion might have followed a questionable call, but the fan's ultimate respect for the Game rarely allowed that to escalate beyond just some inflamed words in the stands... then, back to the Game so as not to miss a minute!

And, in those days, a dad could afford the modest ticket prices (average seat prices were around $1.25) to take the whole family to a day at the Park. In 1965, players, fans, coaches and all the supporting cast knew that this Game was something special and they still treated it that way. The grain of the Game ran true with those folks.

It was a time when most players still needed to work a "regular job" in the off-season to pay their bills. Yes, in the end, professional baseball was a business too, and the pay rates back then reflected that economic reality. In fact, the mean average player salary was $14,341, but the minimum salary was just $3,000 and many players earned that meager rate of pay. Meanwhile, Willie Mays took the top paycheck at $105,000 in 1965. Like I said, if you could play, **you would get paid!** Well, if you could play like Willie!

Still, the players were our heroes and they often became bigger than life through it all. They were the guys that most every kid wanted to be; a Major League Ballplayer. And each of us had our favorites… mine was Number 7 on the Yankees… more on him later!

*   *   *

It was a time when the American and National Leagues consisted of just 10 teams each; there were no "Divisional Play-offs" or "Wild Cards" as there are now. Each team played every other team in their own league 18 games each season. The winner of each League's Pennant from the 162 game season advanced directly to the World Series.

So yes, it was a wonderful, but still a challenging time. Ball players by then were no longer travelling to away games on long train or bus rides, but in exclusive chartered airliners. This new mode of transportation had in fact allowed the Dodgers and Giants to relocate their franchises to the West Coast in 1958, and for even more expansion of Major League teams throughout the country in the coming years.

Players still wore leather shoes with metal cleats riveted to the bottom of them. They came in your choice of black, or black… no matching team colored shoes in those days! And, the players insisted that those mini-houseboats be spit-polished clean daily… sometimes even after batting practice. But no matter what, those shoes were *always* polished after every game and quite frequently before and after the second game of a double header.

Their baseball shoes back then meant a lot to the players and that tradition continues to this day, although for somewhat different reasons. More on that later too. Lots of superstition *and* tradition surrounded this Game!

The uniforms they wore in the colder months were still made of wool and itched something awful and smelled even worse when wet. Makes you wonder how sheep can stand each other during the rainy season!

Oh, the wood in those days, you ask? It was a time when the bats were big and came mostly from Louisville, although some snuck their way into Clubhouses from the Adirondacks… no painted or foreign-made sticks in those days!

And by 1965, advancements in bat manufacturing techniques allowed for a process called "Flame Tempering." That eliminated the need for players (or their Bat Boy for that matter) to use "boning processes" to increase the density of the wood in their bats. The Louisville folks said that this new process "Powerized" their bats. From what I saw, the grain always ran straight and true in those sticks.

A Genuine, Game-Used ("A Gamer") Roger Maris Louisville Slugger.

As resounding proof, the magnitude of the crack of the ball off of Frank Howard's bat one night is something I will never forget. It was thunderous! To this day, I can still hear it ring in my ears as I then knelt just a few feet away. Howard, nick-named "Hondo" and the "Washington Monument" was with the Washington Senators in 1965. At 6'7", 270 pounds (with reportedly just a 32 inch waistline) the four-time All-Star was a mountain of a man and he used some really big and mighty straight lumber when he walked to the plate. Over his long sixteen year career as a player, and fourteen years as a coach and manager, the grain surely ran true in that big fellow!

Frank Howard Used a 37 Inch Long, 35 Ounce Finely-Grained Club.

The players of that era loved the Game and their lumber showed it. No batting gloves in those days... just the raw meat of their hands (with perhaps a bit of sticky pine tar for a better grip or some powdery rosin to dry the sweat) on a tapered stick of wood with which they hoped to smack a three inch leather clad ball (with 108 stitches holding it together) that was being thrown at them from 60 feet 6 inches at ninety miles an hour. What's not to love?

Like today, not all batters were home run threats. Some, like White Sox legend Nelly Fox were "slap hitters" who used what were called "Barrel Bats" that had evolved from the earlier "Bottle Bat." Those sticks had skinny handles, but huge barrel heads. With those oddly shaped bats they would routinely seek to find the tiniest holes in the infield defense to place a hot grounder or a well-spotted low-liner to secure an advance to first base.

1920s Era Bottle Bat Used by Heine Groh Weighed-in at 41 Ounces.

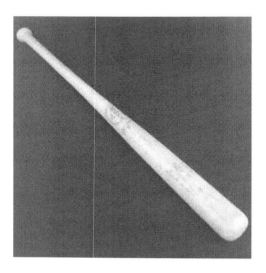

1960s Barrel Bat Used By Slap Hitters.

1965 Jose Cardenal H & B U1 Model Bat.

Some, like the lifetime .275 hitter and long-time coach, Jose Cardenal, used a similar style, but with a thicker handle and without any knob at the end. Players using this type of bat hoped to get comparable results to the Bottle Boys, but with a bit more power. By my recollection, Cardenal broke more bats than anyone in the League that year trying to use the long, extended meat his lumber gave him.

Known as the Louisville U1, those suckers were a full 36 inches long with a barrel 8½ inches in circumference. By comparison, the typical Major Leaguer's bat back then was 34 inches long and 7¼ inches in circumference. Bat weights varied so much it was amazing by today's standards. Some weighed in at today's standard of 32 ounces, while the big sluggers wielded near tree trunks topping the scales at more than an incredible 45 ounces!

Sometime later, with the help of Hillerich & Bradsby (H & B), Cardenal helped to design one of the most popular bat models in professional baseball, the C271. The 271 number designation was picked because it was the 271st model made for a player whose last name began with a "C". Used by the likes of Alex Rodriguez, Ken Griffey, Jr., Cal Ripken, Jr., that design has lasted to this day.

Many power hitters in the 1960s moved to the "Powerized" LS125. Among them were Mickey Mantle, Roger Maris, Harmon Killebrew, Hank Aaron, and Al Kaline of the Detroit Tigers. Boy, there is another great example of a true and gifted player; Mr. Tiger. None ran truer than him.

Mr. Tiger and Hall of Fame Member, Al Kaline.

Whatever their style or model of bat, those boys loved the chance God gave them to play the Game at the highest level. Many of them paid back their God-given gift in kind over their lifetimes. Some players apparently never truly understood the importance of that gift. However, the great ones mostly did. They were like their bats... straight and true, if in some cases, a bit grainy!

Speaking of a "bit grainy" one player still sticks-out in my mind... number 11 and Hall of Fame shortstop, Luis Aparicio, or "Little Louie" as he was known, was that guy.

Louie became the American League Rookie of the Year when he joined the White Sox in 1956 and went on to be a ten time All-Star player. While with the Sox, the combination of him and Nellie Fox remains one of the best double-play combinations in the history of the Game.

Well, in *My Year*, Louie was then with the Baltimore Orioles. Of all the players I met, nobody even came close to rousing a Clubhouse like him!

Whether it be pranks such as running around and snapping

his towel at other player's butts or lacing jock straps with liniment oil, or just his incessant joking (always accompanied with graphic and XXX verbiage for sure) Louie was an absolute fireball, both on and off the field. Some true grain *and grit* ran through that man and he was always fun to watch.

LUIS APARICIO

Little Louie Was Quite the Prankster.

As for the pitching, back then there were pretty much just Starters and Relievers... and no one really wanted to be a Reliever if they could be a Starter. See, back then Starters were *expected* to be their own Closers; meaning they were *expected* to pitch complete games... not that they always did of course, but that was generally the game-plan going in.

Whether a Starter or a Reliever though, you could always tell a pitcher just by walking by them... the pungent aroma of liniment oil rubbed into their shoulders and elbows permeated the air from wherever they were. Just imagine a constant waft of something similar to quadruple strength Ben Gay in your nostrils and you will quickly get the idea. I'll bet all the children sired by those guys must have been conceived in the off-season!

Back then, there really were no Relievers designated as "Long Relievers" or "Middle Relievers" or "Set-up Guys." Nope, in those days the only time you would see a pitching change was if the Starter got hurt, shelled, had a blow-out going against their opponent or a "Specialist" of one type or another was needed to save the day in a game-deciding spot.

In those situations, you just might see a Reliever. See, the Bull Pen was a place where you went when you were a Rookie, a Starter recovering from an injury, a "Specialist" (such as a knuckleballer or a guy who was otherwise known to be tough on a particular type of hitter) or journeyman who could give their team a "few innings" in a mop-up situation.

Premier Knuckleballer, Hoyt Wilhelm.

No, back then the name of the game was strong Starting

Pitching and those who held those roles fought to get and keep them fiercely. For some reason, the name Bob Gibson of the St. Louis Cardinals comes to mind!

Fearsome Fireballer Bob Gibson.

*　　　　*　　　　*

In *My Year*, the Minneapolis Twins (102/60) took the American League Pennant with **My Team**, the Chicago White Sox, coming in Second Place at 95/67. Still, in a way, **every** team in the American League was **My Team** that year. You see, in 1965 I got to meet **all** the players from **all** of the American League teams; and right from White Sox Park. Quite a blessing indeed.

White Sox Park in 1965. Every Fan Loved that Scoreboard and the Boom it Produced on Sox Homers!

The Twins would go on to face the National League winners, the Los Angeles Dodgers (97-65) who by then were well-entrenched in "LALA land" as some called it. But those boys could play and they took the Series 4-3, despite dropping the first two games to the Twins. And why not, with the likes of Sandy Koufax (26-8 with a 2.04 ERA over an incredible 335 regular season innings pitched) and co-Ace Don Drysdale on the mound. Backed by guys like speedster Maury Wills (94 Stolen Bases) on the bases and National League Rookie of the Year, the switch-hitting second baseman Jim Lefebvre in the field, the Dodgers were a formidable foe.

Still, the Twins had extensive offensive power with 4 of the Top 10 hitters in the American League on their squad. Meanwhile, the Dodgers had not one hitter on the National League Top 10 List. Despite the rollercoaster series, Koufax pitched a magnificent complete game shutout on just two days rest in the final game… perhaps good pitching did outweigh good hitting in that seven game series.

*   *   *

It was a time when new American League greats would establish their place in the "Show" as it would become known. The likes of Rookie Tommy John (Yup, the guy for whom the elbow surgery was named), Carl Yastrzemski, Tony Oliva, Joe Pepitone and Bobby Murcer were all on their way to one form of stardom or another.

Somewhat strangely, the not so long enduring Baltimore Oriole outfielder, Curt Blefary won American League Rookie of the Year in 1965 hitting just .260 with 22 home runs. Meanwhile, the equally obscure Zoilo Versalles won MVP honors in the American League that year, leading the League not only in Total Bases, but also in Strikeouts! That, despite the greatness of Al Kaline, Willy Horton, Brooks Robinson, Moose Skowron, Harmon Kilebrew, Bobby Richardson and others who were perennial fan favorites. Funny game, this baseball.

Meanwhile, as mentioned, Lefebvre was the National League Rookie of the Year and the "Say Hey Kid" Willie Mays was their MVP with a .317 average and 52 long ones. Guess he could play some kind of ball, that Mays kid, though I never saw him play in person. I have although seen how he has lived his life on and off the field. The grain sure runs straight in that man!

The "Say Hey Kid" Willie Mays. In 1965,
He Was the Highest Paid Player in Baseball at $105,000.

Sadly, it was a time when Mantle and Maris could no longer compete for home run king titles. The best they could do was struggle to overcome the pain they played with each day they walked onto the field. For Maris, it seemed more mental; for Mantle, it was more physical. Still, it was hard to watch these icons suffer in the ways those men did near the end of their time in the Game. But each day they showed-up and gave all that they had left in their minds, bodies and souls to the Game, and to their fans.

By 1965, Maris seemed to be pretty-well beaten down emotionally from his 1961 feat of surpassing Babe Ruth's all time Regular Season Home Run Record of 60 by 1. The tortuous events of that effort have been well documented, so I will not repeat them here. It is enough to say that 1961 took a mighty toll on Maris.

He didn't play much in 1965 and he seemed to stay pretty much to himself most of the time in the dugout. He died in 1985 at the very early age of 51, but a wonderful memorial was created in his childhood hometown of Fargo, ND to honor his accomplishments. At his request, the museum is open to the public free of charge, everyday of the year except for Christmas, Easter and Thanksgiving. Even under the great strain of his career, it was clear that the grain ran mighty straight in Maris too!

The routine that the Mick went through to get physically ready to play each game was agonizing to watch. The "zippers" on his knees from the multiple surgeries he had endured to repair his injuries looked like grossly constructed spider-webs… made a guy kinda queasy just to look at them!

Still, each day he arrived at the Park early enough so he could get iced, medicated, loosened-up in the steaming whirlpool tub before he finally got "wrapped" and dressed. A few rips in the batting cage and he was good to go… sort of… maybe 60% of his once great peak. But Mickey's 60% was still as good as some players 100%, and he played on.

After the game, more icing, some aspirin with a beer to wash it down and a hot shower, just in time to catch the team bus to the hotel. The next day, it all started over again. And yet, he never refused to take a promotional photo to help the Home Team or a deserving fan.

In 1965, despite all he faced, Mantle still managed to play in 122 games and was again named to the American League All-Star team. Amazingly, he played 144 games in each of his last two Major League years at first base when in 1968, he ended his baseball career. Years later, I had dinner at his Manhattan restaurant, the Central Park South Eatery. While there, I could still feel his presence, although he was long since gone by then. And sadly, now too is the Eatery.

Mickey was always my hero and he will always be tops with

me… and man, check-out his forearms. Thanksgiving Turkeys should be so lucky to have legs with that much meat on them! Nope, nobody surpassed the straightness of his grain.

Maris and Mantle

*   *   *

It was also an era of innovation and ingenious promotions, ala Bill Veeck. He was the first owner to sign an African-American player, Larry Doby to an American League contract. He also signed the oldest Rookie ever to a Major League deal; Satchel Paige was a mere *42 years old* at the time! I would get the opportunity to meet Mr. Paige some seventeen years later and he was still playing the Game at age 59!

Paige began his professional career in 1926 with the Chattanooga Black Lookouts of the Negro Southern League, and played his last professional game on June 21, 1966, for the Peninsula Grays of the Carolina League. In 1959, Paige's mother told a reporter that he was 55 rather than 53, saying she knew this because she wrote it down in her Bible.

Satchel Paige, Warming Up to Pitch for KC at Age 59, or Maybe Even Older. I Took That Pic!

Paige wrote in his autobiography, "Seems like Mom's Bible would know, but she ain't ever shown me the Bible. Anyway, she was in her nineties when she told the reporter that, and sometimes she tended to forget things."

In 1965, Kansas City A's owner Charles O. Finley signed Paige, 59 at the time, for one game. That game included a tribute to several past Negro League players and it was against the Boston Red Sox. He pitched three scoreless innings. I took the picture above as he threw his "Mystery Pitches" in warm-ups one day when he was at Comiskey.

Veeck created the "exploding scoreboard" at Comiskey. He is credited for having announcer Harry Caray sing "Take Me Out to the Ball Game" during the seventh-inning stretch… now a handed-down tradition at the Cub's home park, Wrigley Field where "guest celebrities" still lead the packed crowds in a joyous rendition of that classic to this day.

As a publicity stunt to help celebrate the American League's 50th Anniversary, Bill once hired a player/entertainer to his team who suffered from dwarfism. Eddie Gaedel was his name and he made just one plate appearance in his professional baseball "career." He walked on four consecutive pitches. His uniform jersey with his team number "1/8" on it still resides today in the *National Baseball Hall of Fame and Museum* in Cooperstown, New York. He stood just 3'7" and weighed 65 pounds.

Eddie Gaedel in His One and Only Plate Appearance
in 1951, Ala Mr. Veeck.

Always an innovator, Veeck's worst idea ever came in 1979. It was promoted as "Disco Demolition Night." It was anticipated that an additional 5,000 fans would attend the game that night, bringing with them a vinyl disco album that a local DJ would collect into a large crate and then explode on-field between the double-header games with the Tigers.

However, rather than having an expected total of 25,000 fans, Comiskey Park played host to nearly 50,000 fans that night, many of whom were there just to see the explosion rather than the game itself. So far, so good.

However, after the detonation of the disco records, many fans rushed the field and began throwing the broken records all around in riotous fashion. The field was not only damaged by the explosion, but also by the rowdy fans on the field. Needless to say, the second game had to be cancelled and the visiting Tigers won by a forfeit. I suppose Veeck would say "nothing ventured, nothing gained!"

Fortunately, he had the wisdom not to combine his "Disco Demolition Night" promotion with another great promotion he was known for at Comiskey Park, Ten Cent Beer Night!

Bill Veeck Loved the Game.
He Also Liked to Have a Little Fun at the Park!

For all his zany ways, Bill Veeck remains an icon of the Game. Believe it or not, he spent two years at the same high school my kids would later graduate from, Hinsdale Central High School, located in that cozy little western Chicago suburb. In the end, the Game would not be the way it is today, if not for the true grain of Bill Veeck.

*   *   *

Growing up, radio was still the predominant way we all "saw" games when we were away from the Park. Radio technology had expanded so that table top units were present throughout most people's homes and in their cars by the mid 1950s.

Then a major breakthrough occurred when a tiny electronic component changed everything… it was called a "transistor." It was so small and used so little electricity that it revolutionized a way of life for decades. Now, in a small pocket-sized portable radio, equipped with its dangling little ear plug, millions of baseball fans could listen to a game, almost no matter where they were, as long as they were in range of the transmitter.

A Japanese company, Toshiba, made tons of those little gems and my Dad's mom, Grandma Davis as we called her, once worked building those units at Toshiba's Upstate New York manufacturing plant. We bought a few at a her modest employee discount!

I still love listening to a baseball game today on radio or a computer webcast. I clearly remember listening to some of the great radio broadcasters of the time. The greatest of them all, Vince (Vin) Scully of the Dodgers, is still at it after 66 years. He was a rare baseball radio broadcast treat for a Chicago Area boy.

The Best Ever, Mr. Vin Scully. 66 Years and Still Calling Games.

Bob Elson and Milo Hamilton on WCFL were the ones that mostly filled my head with baseball visions in those days as my Dad and I often listened to their radio broadcasts together while he sipped his evening tea and puffed on his ever-present cigar. Of course, Jack Brickhouse and Lloyd Pettit brought the televised games into our homes, sharing time with the Cubs, on WGN.

By 1965, the baseball and television industries were quickly learning that baseball fans were only too willing to put up with a somewhat fuzzy picture to be able to watch a game from the convenience of their home living room. Sometimes these games were even presented in color! Yup, there was money to be made and TV broadcasts began to expand. In the end, it would be the huge advertising revenues from television that would change the Game forever.

*　　　　*　　　　*

Many kids grow up dreaming that someday they could just set foot on a Major League field. It is the place where dreams are realized, where grown men still get to play a boy's game while getting paid to do so. Heck in those days, many of these players would have done it for little more than meal money and a nice place to sleep. However, the baseball world was in continual flux and the players all had to compete with gusto just to keep their place on the field each and every day. To add to that challenge, the business-side of baseball continued to evolve rapidly. One huge decision that would change the Game forever was the introduction of the first-ever, Major League Baseball Free Agent Amateur League Draft in 1965.

The top pick in that famous Draft was Arizona State Sophomore, Rick Monday. That year, Monday and teammate Reggie Jackson lead the Sun Devils to the 1965 College World Series Championship over Ohio State. Rick batted .359 that season and was named College Player of the Year.

While he had a very successful 19 year professional career playing for the Athletics, Cubs and Dodgers, it was his over-the-top patriotic act in Los Angeles years later for which he will always be most remembered.

It was is the first inning of the Cubs versus the Dodgers game on April 25, 1976, when two alleged war protesters (a father with his eleven-year-old son) ran onto the outfield and tried to set fire to an American flag that they had brought with them. Monday, who was an outfielder with the visiting Cubs at the time, saw what was happening and bolted towards the pair and grabbed the flag away from the would-be anarchists.

To the roar of the crowd, Rick ran the flag over to the Los Angeles pitcher while the ballpark police officers arrested the two intruders. When he came to bat in the next half-inning, Rick got a standing ovation from the crowd and the big message board behind the left-field bleachers in the stadium flashed the message, "RICK MONDAY... YOU MADE A GREAT PLAY..."

Monday later said, "If you're going to burn the flag, don't do it around me. I've been to too many veterans' hospitals and seen too many broken bodies of guys who tried to protect it." By the way, Rick still has the flag he rescued from the protesters; he has been offered up to $1 million to sell it, but has declined all offers.

Yes, the grain ran true in Rick Monday on that special day, and it still does today as he handles the play-by-play duties of the Dodgers radio broadcasts.

Other notable picks in the first-ever Major League Baseball Free Agent Amateur League Draft in 1965 were future Hall of Famers, Johnny Bench, Nolan Ryan and Tom Seaver, although Seaver opted to return to USC rather than accept an offer from the Dodgers that year.

Also selected in the initial Draft were future All-Stars Sal Bando, Ray Fosse, Kenny Holtzman and Gene Tenace among others. Tenace would also take MVP honors in the 1972 World Series for the Oakland A's.

Rick Monday, Major League Baseball's Top Draft Pick in 1965.

*   *   *

Many temptations faced the players in those days, just like today. However, the lure of the Game (and some mighty tight behavior rules imposed by the owners and the Leagues) helped keep most of them straight and true... and highly focused.

Some, like the intensely driven Red Sox rising star, Tony Conigliaro (AKA, Tony C as I knew him) lost his well anticipated chance at mega-stardom when in 1967 a fastball shattered his face and destroyed the vision in his left eye. Today's "flapped" helmet might have saved him. But, despite valiant comeback attempts, tragedy now filled his once brilliant life, and he perished in 1990, reportedly the result of a stroke that had put him into a coma for many years. The Game gives and the Game takes.

In 2006, the Red Sox added a 200-seat bleacher section on top of the right field roof, and named it "Conigliaro's Corner" in his honor. More on Tony C a bit later. You won't believe that story!

As with the Cub's Ron Santo, deserved acknowledgements sometimes come too late. Ron lived a life that exemplified the truest and straightest of human fiber. His legacy lives on.

Chicago Cubs Third Baseman, Ron Santo. He was Posthumously Voted into the Hall of Fame in 2012.

I am very glad to say that I got to see Santo bat in person once too, along with the other Cub greats that year. No, official inter-league play did not exist back then, but each year the two Chicago teams, the White Sox and Cubs would hold a charity event and play each other to the delight of the fans. In *My Year*, they played that game on the south side of town at Comiskey, and I had a big role to fill that night… and, boy was I ever proud of that.

*   *   *

Well, I was never a great player, but for one magical season I got to be on wonderful ball fields side-by-side with many of the baseball elite of an era. No, not as a player, but as an important part of the Show.

To be clear, back then baseball was more than just something "to do." It was **our** National Pastime. It was part of the very fabric and grain of **our** nation. It was not just a reflection on our way of life, it was **part** of our way of life… thus, the reason for the historical background I provided herein. With that in mind, to be a component of that great spectacle at any level was truly a blessing. After all, it was *the* Game.

Yes, as you probably guessed by now, not only was I a Major League Bat Boy in 1965, more importantly I was chosen by the Chicago White Sox to be their ***Visiting Team Bat Boy*** that year. Quite an honor indeed!

That meant I would get to meet *all* of the great American League players of that era. What's more, over that glorious season I gained a wealth of experiences that would later help me grow into manhood, with memories to last a lifetime.

This is my story about *Then and Now*. It is a journey that I hope you will relive with me and I will do my best not to disappoint. You see, in that one incredible year, for me the Grain Ran True.

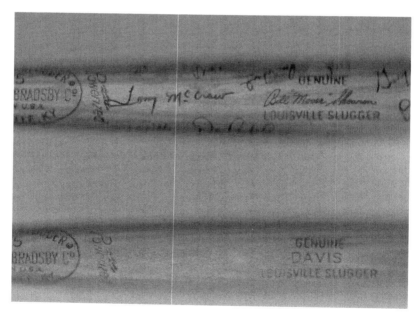

Player-Autographed "Moose" Skowron Bat and My Own, Genuine Louisville Slugger.

HOW IT BEGAN

One day in early March, 1965, my Dad arrived home to our north suburban abode carrying with him a copy of the Chicago Daily News. As had become a custom, each year the News, in conjunction with the White Sox, sponsored a contest to choose the Home and Visiting Team Bat Boys (and field assistants) for the coming season. Most other teams in those days gave those honors to kids who were friends of management or the like, so this was kind of a big opportunity... especially for a young Sox fan!

Well, my Dad quickly passed along the Sports Section and suggested that I check out the advertisement for the contest. Although I was a diehard Sox fan for a fourteen year old, we did live in the northern suburbs and most folks around there in those days were Cub's fans... including my mother!

So, going in I didn't really think I would have much of a shot at winning this thing. And, even if I did, how on earth would I, a fourteen year old kid, be able to get myself all the way to the South Side of Chicago (about twenty-five miles away from my home) on nearly a daily basis for the six month season? And even more challenging was that the area around the ballpark was known back then almost as much for its "Low Income Tenement Projects" (AKA "Ghettos in the Sky") as for its professional baseball Park. No, this was not going to be an easy task. But "what the heck" I said, at least I could try. Besides, the rewards were tantalizing:

- A regular salary ($6 per game, $8 for a Double Header!)
- A $1000 Scholarship for First Place, $500 for Second Place.
- An all expenses paid road trip with the Sox aboard their

31

private airliner to New York, Detroit and Cleveland (For both the Home and Visiting Team Bat Boys.)
- Free car parking and home game tickets for my family.
- And of course, the chance of a lifetime to be a Sox Bat Boy for the entire season!

The contest rules were pretty clear and fairly simple; but not really that easy to execute. The main challenge was that each contestant needed to write a letter using fifty words or less as to why they wanted to be the Sox Bat Boy. So much to say, in so little space.

Luckily, my Dad had an idea and a good one. What he suggested was to keep the brief opening heading I had already drafted, but then to write the words

W-H-I-T-E S-O-X

in bold letters vertically down the left side margin of the paper. Then for each letter, I could write a brief statement starting with that letter... B-R-I-L-L-I-A-N-T... even for a dad!

So, off I went:

Would like working with players

Have chance to meet sportscasters

Interested in sports

Travel with team

Employment later as sportscaster

Sure Sox will win pennant

Opportunties afforded

X, hmmm... but what could I come up with for that problematical letter "X" in the word "Sox"? I thought it over, conferred with friends and family and finally came up with:

X-ray talents of players. Yup, that would do the trick.

Below is a copy of the original letter that I sent to the Chicago Daily News in March 1965, now a little worse for wear. Count 'em, exactly fifty words on the dot! Now the dream was set in motion.

Why I Want to be a White Sox
Bat Boy in 1965

Would like working with players.
Have chance to meet sportscasters.
Interested in sports.
Travel with team.
Employment later as sportscaster.

Sure Sox will win pennant
Opportunities offered.
X-ray talents of players.

Would I make a good representation?
Have made honor roll, played baseball
six years, and have been Scout leader.

Then one day after school in early April, when I had nearly forgotten about the Bat Boy contest all together, my Mom set a clean, white and neatly typewritten envelope addressed to me on the kitchen table in front of me as I munched on my daily pack of Twinkies. I opened that envelope from the Chicago Daily News with half-hearted emotions, expecting by that late date that I had probably only received a thank-you or recognition letter for entering the contest.

However, to my complete astonishment, it was an invitation. The invitation was from the Daily News promotional department requesting that my Mom, Dad and I attend a special luncheon that coming Saturday at Comiskey Park. It seemed that I had been chosen as one the top fifteen finalists in the 1965 Chicago Daily News-Chicago White Sox Bat Boy Contest! The letter also notified me that I had already earned a 1965 White Sox season pass and a baseball autographed by the entire team. But that was just the start.

As you can see from that letter, my parents and I were invited to that luncheon so that I and the other candidates could compete in person for the Bat Boy positions. While there, we would also get a tour of the Park and have lunch with one of the judges in the elite Bards Room dining section. Each kid would then be interviewed one-by-one by a distinguished panel of judges, with the winners being announced on the spot. Wow, it is hard to express the excitement we all felt as I passed that crisp, beautiful letter around the kitchen table for all to enjoy.

And here is that letter from Mr. Pecoraro.

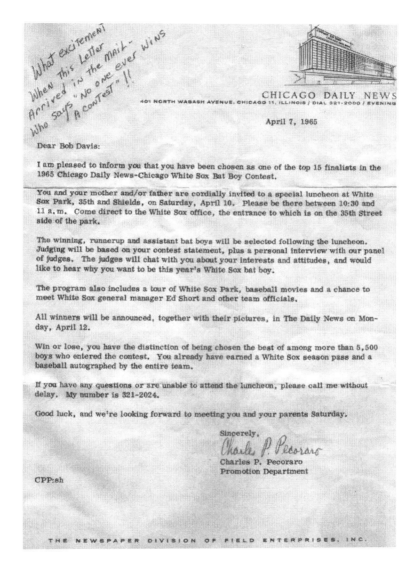

So, it was with anxious excitement that my folks and I headed to the icon of American League baseball in Chicago, Comiskey Park. Donning a new sport coat for the occasion, I was now ready to meet the challenge ahead.

The Woodland Bards Trophy Room at Comiskey Park.

Upon arrival, I was honored to be seated with Hall of Fame Member, Ray Schalk. Known mostly for his great defense and mental toughness in guiding pitchers as the Sox catcher for most of his career, Mr. Schalk was a very nice man to us that Saturday in April, 1965.

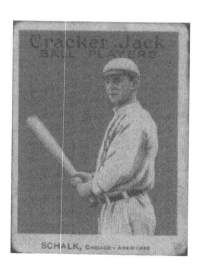

Ray Schalk, White Sox catcher, Hall of Fame 1955,
18 Seasons With the Sox.

After lunch, each prospective Bat Boy was taken in turn into the Sox Board Room which was adjacent to the Bard's Room, for their personal interview. Meanwhile, the other contestants and their parents waited nervously in the main seating area of the Bards Room, watching old silent baseball highlight reels from the 1920s, the 1930s, the 1940s, and… you get the picture.

Well, that quickly became a long, tedious and nerve-wracking experience as each one of the fifteen boys was individually interviewed for about 10 to 15 minutes each. And the judges were not just regular folk. Nope, like Mr. Schalk, this was an august panel comprised of Chicago business, sports and political leaders. In fact, the Honorable Richard J. Daley, Mayor of Chicago was scheduled to attend, but was a late cancellation.

An Impressive Selection Panel for Sure!

Waiting, and not so patiently, my turn came after about eight others had their interview. Naturally, I was a bit nervous going into this bastion of baseball lore, but I had sized up the competition and figured I had at least a decent chance of winning a spot somewhere on the field. You see, every finalist had already earned a season pass to the Sox home games. Ten kids would actually win something more and six kids would earn the prized spots on the field for the entire 1965 Season.

The remaining four boys would be given all expenses paid trips to the Sox Boys Baseball Camp in Wisconsin.

Well, I liked Wisconsin and all, but my eye was not on that prize; I wanted to win that Number One spot, Home Team Bat Boy for the 1965 Chicago White Sox!

So, as I entered the room I put on a big smile and introduced myself. Mr. Schalk was kind of like my sponsor and he gave a bit of background on me to the others. And then the questions began.

"How long have you been playing baseball?" "What subjects do you like most in school?" "How are your grades?" and "Who are your favorite players?" The questions kept on rolling and I kept on answering!

While I responded to each question directly, I also tried to inject a bit of humor along the way. One judge nearly boxed me in though when he exhorted "Well, Bob we heard a rumor that coming from up North that you are really a Cubs fan... what say you to that young man?"

I immediately stood up from my chair, looked him squarely in the eye and said "Oh no sir, that's my Mother! I have always been a Sox fan." Boy did that draw a laugh from that well-healed panel of gentlemen! I then went on to explain that "My father came from New York and all my relatives are Yankee fans... except for my Dad and me. We're both bound to the White Sox!"

Well, that was that. I left the room feeling pretty good about the interview, but now, the wait began anew. An hour went by as the remaining boys went and returned. Meanwhile, the rest of us had to wait quietly in the Bard's Room watching those old subtitled baseball newsreels from days gone by... hmmm, not quite as much fun as it sounded in Mr. Pecoraro's letter!

Then another hour slowly passed as the last boy finished his interview. And then, more waiting as the judges deliberated. By now, it was late afternoon and the tension in the room was so thick that you could have stood on it. Then finally... the selections were announced.

I was never the most confident kid, but I felt pretty sure that Wisconsin was not in my future! Sure enough, those kid's names were called and they came and went, leaving just the six field slots.

"And in Sixth place and Visiting Team Ball Boy, Gregory Driskell!" "One down, five to go" I thought. Then, "In Fifth place and Home Team Ball Boy, George Sims!"

Okidoki, onward we go. "In Fourth place and Assistant Visiting Team Bat Boy, Luke (AKA Pat) Ivers!"

Now a little bit of doubt set in as my stomach began to churn and my heart raced. "What if I didn't even make it at all? That one kid over there looks pretty old for his age and that other kid next to him is already sixteen years old and he's looking mighty confident."

"And our Third Place winner and Assistant Home Team Bat Boy... Tom Brzezinski!" Whew, that older looking kid took Third... glad he's out of the way!

Then, much like the Miss America Contest, the Master of Ceremonies went through all the language about the roles of the First and Second Place Winners and all the great stuff coming their way.

"And now, in Second Place and your 1965 Visiting Team Bat Boy..." "Wait a minute" I thought, did he just say Bob Davis? "No, I was going to be in First place... What happened? He must have somehow read it wrong" I thought. But as people cheered and applauded, the MC said "And your First Place Winner and 1965 Home Team Bat Boy, Fred Croft!"

Wow, while thirteen other guys were majorly envious of me, I somehow felt a devastating letdown. It may sound like I was an ungrateful, spoiled brat for feeling defeated in my *own* victory, but not being Number One was remarkably painful for a competitive young man hoping to make his mark. I should have been jumping for joy, but in my mind at that particular moment, I felt like just the best of the losers.

Naturally, my parents were overjoyed and so proud of their son. I tried to put up a good front, but as we hopped back into our powder blue, 1961 Buick Skylark for the long ride back north, a tear did well-up in my eyes. Thankfully, it was dark outside and I covered my sadness, slumping in the back seat feigning a nap after my long day, so as not to spoil that big moment for Mom and Dad.

My folks never really understood those youthful emotions I had that day, but at least my usually frugal Dad decided to spring for a big dinner at the best fried chicken place around, Phil Johnson's in nearby Northbrook. Good food always had a way of cheering me up!

Now Long Gone, Phil Johnson's Was a Family Favorite. Another Favorite Was Hackney's in Glenview. It's Still There!

In the coming days, weeks and months, I would come to understand that my Second Place Win was actually the greatest of all gifts. What I and many other contestants had not fully appreciated at first was that as the Visiting Team Bat Boy I would be carrying the bats of **all** the American League players, not just the White Sox players like the guys on the Home Team Side! That meant that Mantle, Maris, Kaline, Oliva, Kilebrew, Colavito, Yastrzemski and **all** the other greats of the day were mine! Even better because I got to hang with the Sox players during batting and fielding practice too, not to mention the Road Trip I would still be going on!

And other than a bit smaller scholarship and not quite the initial prestige, I got all the same perks as the Number 1 guy. Not to diminish Fred's win in any way as he deserved it, but this coming in Second Place thing was suddenly a pretty great deal. Sometimes in life, being where you *belong* to be is better than being where you thought you *wanted* to be. God does work in funny ways and that is a lesson I have carried with me since.

The coming months would bring with them things I could not even begin to imagine. Being part of the White Sox organization was an amazing fire hose of experiences and emotions. Not all of what was to come would be fun or even pleasant. However, as I would later realize, all that did come my way had a reason and a purpose behind it, along with a few unexpected challenges too… just like the great Game itself.

My first day walking into Comiskey as an employee and not as a spectator was chilling. Now the greatness of this chapter in my life was about to really sink in and on that day I thanked my lucky stars for my good fortune.

Just more wonderful experiences that made 1965 a very special year; a year when the grain of the Game still ran true.

Davis (left) and Croft watch infield practice.

One of Many Promotional Photos Taken That Magical Year!

A DAY IN THE LIFE
OF LUMBER MEN

B eing a Bat Boy back in *My Year* was a little different than it is today, but for the most part it was generally the same. However, becoming a Bat Boy for a Major League team as the result of a contest did have its own challenges. Accordingly, what follows is a little glimpse into the various jobs and roles of the Chicago White Sox 1965 Visiting Team Bat Boy Crew.

First-off, most people assume that Visiting Team Bat Boys travel with the team. That was (and is today) largely not the case as most home teams provided the visiting team with a Bat Boy for their stay. The traveling team provided a matching team uniform for the provided Bat Boy (me) but not for the Assistant (Pat) or for the Ball Boy (Greg) who would don their usual White Sox uniforms, as pictured.

The 1965 Chicago White Sox Visiting Team Bat Boy Crew.
L-R: Pat Ivers (Assistant Bat Boy), Greg Driskell (Ball Boy),
Bob Davis (Bat Boy)

Going in, most people don't spend much of their time at a ballpark watching the Bat Boys. That's how it should be. The Bat Boys are there in support of the players and generally, the less visible the better. However, that was not the same for the Ball Boys.

The Ball Boys, who patrolled the field level sidelines, had a huge public relations job ahead of them each game. Firstly, they needed to protect the fans from scorching foul balls hit down the line and to retrieve those ricocheted bullets from the field of play as quickly as possible when that happened.

Secondly, they needed great people skills in handling the nearby box-seated fans who were constantly pleading to be given one of those foul balls! Yes, Ball Boys (and now Ball Girls and even older gents at some parks) *are* a highly visible and important part of the Game. Moreover, let's not forget that a lot of those line drives headed their way are traveling at 100 MPH or more. I tip my cap to those folks. Greg Driskell , our Visiting Team Ball Boy, did a first-rate job with all of those responsibilities.

The main responsibility of the Assistant Bat Boy in *My Year* was to keep everything in the dugout in order. Pat (Luke) Ivers, fulfilled that role perfectly throughout the season.

By the way, Pat's first name was Luke, but he preferred to go by his nickname "Pat" which was derived from his middle name Patrick, as I recall. By coincidence, the same kind of thing went for me. My first name is Glenn, but until I went away to college, I was known as "Bob" which was derived from my middle name Robert. These days, only my Uncle Bob, my Aunt Gertie's husband, still calls me Bob, or actually Bobby, and it doesn't bother me in the slightest coming from him!

The main responsibilities of the Bat Boy were to make sure that the other crew members had done their jobs. Then it was his job to tend to everything around the Batter's Circle and to retrieve the hitter's bats when they ended their session at the plate. Once I retrieved the bat, I would hand it off to Pat who would put it away in the bat case. I would then head back to the Batter's Circle to assist the next batter. Yup, that's me pictured to the right of the Batter's Circle, ready to retrieve my next bat.

Bob Tending the Batter's Circle for KC Outfielder, Mike Hershberger.

The home plate umpires were responsible for the game balls. Before each game they would prepare a whole bunch, about 6 dozen I guessed, by rubbing them with a special mud retrieved exclusively from the Delaware River. Officially designated as "Baseball Rubbing Mud" it would give the balls a slightly rougher surface, thereby improving the grip for the pitcher. Believe it or not, this same practice continues today, using that same Mud from the Delaware River on the New Jersey side. Talk about long-standing traditions!

The umpire would then give the prepped balls to the Home Team Equipment Manager. He in turn would dole them out to the Home Team Bat Boy or the Assistant for delivery to the ump as needed, usually three or four balls at a time, just like today.

I do not recall if the umpires were as quick to toss balls out after hitting the dirt as they are today, but they sure went through that six dozen balls quickly… always seemed like a waste to me! I mean if a ball got hit on the button resulting in a ground ball out, the ball was routinely tossed back to the pitcher for continued use. However, if a pitch even slightly clipped the dirt on its way to the catcher, the ump would immediately toss the ball out, or on occasion, pocket it for further inspection later.

One thing for sure was that pitchers in those days could do amazing things to change the spin of a pitch with even the slightest abrasion or the application of even the tiniest of foreign substances to a ball. (Satchel Paige and a fellow named Gaylord Perry were known to be among the best at doing that little bit of ball doctoring.) At first, I thought maybe that was why the umpires so quickly discarded pitched balls. But actually, there is quite a story behind all of this and I will address that in a later chapter, so please stay tuned for that.

In the end though, those one time gamers (a ball or a bat used in an actual game) would be repurposed as batting practice balls anyway. So, maybe it all does make sense, especially once you know the story behind the "dirty ball era" of baseball.

* * *

Most days the three of us, the Visiting Team Bat Boy Crew, would get to the ballpark about 2 ½ hours before the game. The first order of business was to get into our uniforms and then get a bite to eat. Most of the weekday games had a 7 PM first-pitch, so a nice snack beforehand was more than a treat… it was our dinner. And any dessert would often not come until after midnight on those game nights.

The White Sox always provided sandwiches to us at no charge up in the Bards Room. They would supply the same to the players between games on double-header days or if there was a weather delay. We were free to buy stuff from the vendors too before game time if we so chose.

Usually the vendor's fare was better than the ham sandwiches in the Bards room. So if I had an extra buck or so, I might opt for that. One guy made really good burgers and popcorn, so his became my favorite stand to visit. Of course everyone knows how good Chicago-style hot dogs are, especially at the ballpark, so I sure had my share of those "Vienna Red-Hots" as well.

About two hours prior to game time, our Crew brought-out all of Visiting Team's equipment to the dugout from inside the Clubhouse. Each starting player had 2 bats that were marked with their number on the knob. Pat would store them in a big, "pigeon hole" type box which made it easy and quick for him retrieve a new stick if the batter broke the one he was using during his at-bat. There was another big box with pigeon holes for holding batting helmets. They were also marked with the player's number, but on the back of the helmet.

The main stock of bats was kept by the Visiting Team Equipment Manager in the Clubhouse. He had to keep all that stuff up-to-date inventory-wise and have it ready to ship on to the next destination on get-away-day. That was the same for all of the back-up equipment, except most catchers personally kept three mitts with them. One was for game use and the other two for "breaking in" at various stages.

The player's personal items were their responsibility in the dugout. No batting gloves then, so just their sun glasses, fielding gloves, etc. Occasionally, if the weather changed quickly, we might have to run a set of sun glasses out to a fielder during an inning, so we also had to be on our toes to help with that when needed.

All of this preparation and activity was performed in the field of play, in foul territory of course, but still very much in play. Today, for safety sake, the Bat Boys are far removed from the on-deck batter and usually sit on a chair near the edge of the dugout, protected of course with a dual-side earflap batting helmet. That is undoubtedly a modern-day concession to appease the team's legal staff, but not so much in *My Year...* just a regular woolen baseball cap topped our heads!

The key to a well functioning dugout is to make sure that the various pieces of equipment, especially the bats, were where they belonged at all times. Nothing brings down the heat faster than the Bat Boys wasting time looking for a replacement bat when a player breaks his gamer on a foul ball. Fans don't like it, the players *really* don't like it and your boss majorly doesn't like it. In our case, our boss was the Clubhouse Manager and he went by the most appropriate name, Sharkey. Let me explain.

Sharkey was a scrappy little fellow who grew-up on the streets of Chicago and he had a cigar permanently attached to his lips. Clearly, his sense of humor did not run very deep. I thought I saw him smile once. But then again, that was probably just wishful thinking!

Sharkey made it pretty clear from the get-go that he didn't take too kindly to having three more "God Damn Contest kids" working in ***His*** Clubhouse. Nope, if he had his way, he would have been doing the hiring of his own staff and he for darn sure would not have been on the panel of nine judges that picked us. After all, this fella had worked for the White Sox in one capacity or another since 1906 (including as a Bat Boy) so I would imagine he figured that he had a pretty fine idea of what made for a good Bat Boy, contest or not.

Our Boss and Visiting Team Clubhouse Manager, Sharkey. His Career With the Sox Spanned 61 Years.

The White Sox Visiting Team Clubhouse was physically up-to-date and really nice... much nicer than the ones that I would later see on my road trip to New York, Detroit and Cleveland.

Sharkey ran **everything** in that Clubhouse like a Swiss watch. He made sure the cooler was always stocked with the specific beverages that each team favored. Hamm's and Pabst Blue Ribbon were big favorites, as was the non-alcoholic, Green River! He made sure that each player's locker was set-up just the way the player wanted it. He did his research and he kept notes... forever.

Some Clubhouse Favorites With the Players and Coaches.

Sharkey made sure that the toilet and bath areas had all the right soaps, shaving equipment, aftershave lotion, etc., and he was always on top of special requests. Need a quick sandwich, you got it. Need a fresh pack of smokes, you got it. Need a special favor of most any kind, well Sharkey was your man. He might get an underling to do the dirty work, but he always, and I mean *always* collected any gratuity that resulted.

You see, Sharkey and his fellow Clubhouse Managers across the Major Leagues made a tidy little sum on the side by receiving tips from the players, coaches and the King of the Show, the team's Manager. As you might imagine, Sharkey wasn't too much into sharing. If a Crew Member earned a tip, it had to be from something Sharkey either couldn't do or didn't want to provide. That usually boiled down to something a Crew Member did above and beyond the call of duty while on the field to assist a player or a coach.

Sharkey hated going into the dugout or anywhere near the field. Despite his many years working for the Sox, I am not sure he even liked baseball. That was OK by us, because once we left the Clubhouse we were more or less on our own, unless something went wrong. However, you better never let anything go **so** wrong as to get Sharkey walking towards you down the tunnel that connected the Clubhouse to the dugout. How amazing then, especially by today's standards, that we three fourteen year old kids were almost completely autonomous once we stepped into the dugout and on to the field. Pretty sure that wouldn't be the case today!

Aside from having a "great" guy like Sharkey as our boss, one really nice perk of the job was that we got to keep the bats that the players broke while hitting. On the Visiting side, we just took turns between the crew. Each of us got about an equal number of bats over the course of the season, which worked out just fine for all of us.

I ended up with somewhere around fifty or so broken sticks by season's end. A few of mine were really special. I scored a Roger Maris cracked gamer (pictured previously) a Brooks Robinson cracked gamer, a Joe Adcock cracked gamer (all in great condition) and several Jose Cardenal bats in various states of condition... man that guy sure broke a lot of bats!

Sadly, I am not exactly sure what other bats I had collected during the season. Although they were once proudly displayed at my parent's home and then "safely" stored away there, something went awry. You see, as I mentioned previously, my Dad was a frugal man by most every measure. One winter after I was grown and living on my own in a small apartment somewhere, Dad decided that he could save a few bucks on firewood and began digging into my stored-away prizes.

Not sure what Dad was thinking, but one by one, my treasured ASH's were quickly becoming nothing more than ASHES... luckily I got to them when I did or they all might have been reduced to cinders. Little did he apparently know that those pieces of lumber would one day be worth far more than the value of the kindling wood he could have purchased in town. By today's pricing, even a minor-level star's broken bat could be worth at least a few hundred dollars at auction... ones like my Maris bat sell for many thousands. Luckily, that baby escaped the inferno!

Reaping that kind of reward would have also been the case with a Tony Conigliaro batting helmet I retrieved after he smashed it into three pieces after making his fourth ground-out to the shortstop one day. He was a strong boy that Tony, and very passionate (uh, hot-tempered at times, perhaps!)

Well, that gem didn't get burned, just tossed away in the garbage, assumed to be a piece of junk during some home remodeling project. Given Tony's later accident, I can't even imagine what that bit of memorabilia would be worth today to a diehard Boston Fan. However, aside from the monetary value, I am really sorry that prize met such a sorrowful fate; just like its original owner. I am more guarded with my irreplaceable stuff these days.

*   *   *

In *My Year*, after the equipment was delivered and organized, it was our free-time for a while. For my crew, that usually meant running to the outfield to shag balls during batting practice. Strangely though, we had very little interaction with our cohorts across the way. It was as though there was a line down the middle of the field and we rarely crossed over to the opposite dugout, and vice versa with them. In fact, I had more conversations with the White Sox players than I did with my peers across the way… not sure why that was. Perhaps Home Team Bat Boy Fred ran his crew a little differently than I did in the Visitors' dugout. I just don't know, but we sure had some fun on our side!

Without any apparent concern about any kind of legal liability back then, the Sox coaches and management seemed only too happy to have us prancing around out there helping to retrieve those Batting Practice (BP) balls. However, many outfielders from both teams liked to use that time to hone their fielding skills, to get a feel for the Park and its nuances or to just run wind-sprints. Just one more thing for us to keep in mind so that we didn't get in the players way. One thing was always clear, you never wanted to get in a player's way… never!

Another thing really important to keep in mind when in the outfield during BP was that the balls coming at you were being hit by very strong, very talented grown men who could put a lot of hurt on a ball. Upon witnessing the incredible speed and spin on those balls coming at you, one quickly realized that you were not in Kansas anymore, Toto!

After a while, we kind of got the hang of BP outfield play. By mid-summer, I actually began to feel pretty confident in my ability to catch those rockets coming my way. I was a pretty big kid at 6 foot, 180 pounds and was often mistaken for a player, especially in my Visiting Team Uniform. So, one Sunday afternoon before a game with the Tigers, for some reason still unbeknownst to me, I decided to give the infield a try for a change. Not such a good idea in hindsight!

Well, as I strolled from deep left field towards the shortstop position, everything seemed like it was kind of cool. "Maybe I could play the infield someday" I thought to myself. However, not two seconds after I stepped on the dirt between second and third, a crack off of future Hall of Famer Al Kaline's bat sent a laser bolt directly at my head.

The speed and hooking action on that spiraling baseball is something I simply cannot describe. It was like a heat-seeking missile and my head seemed to be providing the warmth it needed to lock-on. Frozen in my tracks with no time to react, I saw my complete short life pass before my eyes and then in an instant, it was there. NOOO! At the last millisecond, I tilted my head sharply to the right and that high-speed torpedo passed within an inch of my left ear.

All I can remember was how big that ball appeared as it honed in on me and how blazingly loud those raised seams sang as it whirled on by me, miraculously and now harmlessly falling onto the grass in left field. Several players saw what had just happened. They were almost as frightened for me as I was for myself. No words needed to be said. I simply began walking backwards, swiftly now, back to the relative safety of the outfield... the deepest part of the outfield in fact, never to return to the infield during BP. Thankfully, the Detroit uniform pants they provided were dark in color to camouflage the unfortunate result of my, um… excitement from that moment. Ah just kidding. Nope, I was too scared after that to poop for weeks!

*   *   *

Also, during the hour or so before game time, many pitchers would concurrently come onto the outfield grass to exercise, to throw long-toss and/or to run their sprints. Sometimes, they would ask us to stand guard for them while they did that. In some cases they would want us to join them as they ran… both "tip able" duties, should they so choose to do so.

In one case, one memorable player always had me play long-toss with him every time he came to town. His name was Phil Ortega and he pitched for the Washington Senators in 1965.

Phil Ortega

Filomeno Coronado Ortega, AKA Phil, pitched in the "Bigs" for about ten years. He was of Yaqui Indian decent, born in Gilbert, AZ and raised near Phoenix. He was never a super star in the record books, but he loved his life as a professional baseball player and he always showed his appreciation for that privilege.

Yup, every time the Senators came to town, he would flag me down and we would head out to right field. First we would stretch, then we would run and then we would throw.

Can you imagine how that felt to a fourteen year old boy to be asked to play catch with a Major League pitcher? I was in heaven and I can never thank Mr. Ortega enough for those times.

And you know the real kicker? On get-away-day each trip he would slip me $5. On the last series of the year it was $50! I mean in 1965 that was some serious dough. Remember, I made only $6 in wages for the whole game!

Naturally, I tried to refuse his gifts, but he would hear nothing of it and insisted I take the money each time. He just said he could play catch with those other guys (his teammates) anytime. To him he was just paying back to the Game… What a guy. Thank you, Sir Ortega… No doubt how the grain ran in that man!

*　　　　*　　　　*

So, as the game was about to start, Greg would take his place sitting in a folding chair down the right field Line, ready to protect and cajole with the excited fans. Pat would make sure that the dugout was in good order and ready to go. And I would carry a weighted bat, a pine tar rag and a rosin bag out to the Batter's Circle where I would kneel down on a pad nearby to assist the batter with anything else he might need. Now, the game could begin!

As I have mentioned previously, some players were highly superstitious and some were extra particular. Those guys could make quite a stink if my Crew or I broke any of their known or unknown rules. You might get cut some slack during the first few games of the year when that team visited your ballpark, but not so much after that.

One such player was Rocky Colavito and he was known as "The Rock." He was a stellar corner outfielder for the Cleveland Indians in *My Year*, but not much of conversationalist around the Batter's Circle. Let me digress for a moment.

Rocky Colavito

Rocky hailed from the Bronx in New York and he was a pretty intense guy. He was a very good player, very strong, a nine-time All-Star and later was a 2006 inductee into the Cleveland Indians Baseball Hall of Fame. The thing was that Rocky hated pine tar. He hated the look and feel of it. And, he hated the smell of it even more. So, when he was "In the Hole," job-one for me as the Bat Boy was to hide the pine tar rag after the On Deck batter had used it.

Well, I had been given a heads-up about this situation and routinely took the appropriate precautions. However, during mid-season, Pat, my Assistant, took a turn on the field while I tended to the dugout duties for a change.

Now, I had reminded him about Rocky before the game, but I guess he either forgot or lost track of the line-up and… oops, that pine tar rag lay right next to number 21 on that Circle as he knelt down to wait his turn at the plate. That sure didn't go over too well as Pat got the stare of death from "The Rock." I took over at his next at bat and all was forgiven I guess, as we did not hear anything more about from Sharkey.

Many years later, Colavito coached for the Cleveland Indians in the 1970s and then the Kansas City Royals in the early to mid 1980s. In 1983, when Rocky was a coach for the Royals, he had an extremely bizarre and interesting run-in with pine tar.

It is awfully ironic that a man with such distaste for that sticky stuff would get ejected from a game for defending it. But yes, this was the famous George Brett Pine Tar game and here is what happened.

The Rock and Royals' Manager Dick Howser vehemently argued against Rookie Home Plate Umpire Tim McClelland's decision to disallow a two-run home run just hit by George Brett. This decision was based on Yankees' Manager Billy Martin's frivolous protest that the pine tar on Brett's bat went past the Trade Mark label; a potentially minor cosmetic infraction that in reality would not have aided Brett's homer in the least.

The Infamous George Brett Pine Tar Bat.

That decision temporarily nullified the home run that had come with two-outs in the top-half of the ninth inning at Yankee Stadium, that would have yielded the Royals a 5-4 lead. Rocky, Brett and Howser were ejected from the game due to their, um, let's say, overly expressive discussion with the ump.

Once known as the "home run that lost a game," American League President Lee MacPhail eventually overruled the rookie Umpire's decision and restored Brett's home run. The game was restarted a month later in mid-August and officially ended with the Royals winning 5-4.

Guess ol' Rock learned to be OK with that stinky, goopy and sticky stuff, as long as it was going to help the team's cause and it wasn't on *his* bat!

∗   ∗   ∗

So, now the game was underway and I was doing my thing. Each time I retrieved a player's bat, I would hand it to Pat who did his thing and filed it safely away. Meanwhile, Greg was down the line doing his thing… keeping the fans safe and well-charmed.

Many days were pretty much like that. Most of the players didn't interact too much with any of us during the game, other than to ask for something when they needed it.

One time though just before a game, one player asked *me* if *I* would like to try something he had… a little "Chaw" as he called it. Well, that little Chaw was actually Redman Chewing Tobacco and I fell for the bait. Taking a nice big wedge between my thumb and forefinger, I popped that baby right into my mouth. I took a large bite of that wad and swallowed the bitter juice it produced thinking "No more bubble gum for me, now I had become a man!"

Well, that thought lasted about ten seconds before that nicotine blast hit my brain and my stomach at the same time. Whoa!!!! Holly Cow… Oh My God! That was some explosion inside me and my dash to the bathroom to rid myself of that stuff was intense. The culprit, power hitting Detroit Tigers first baseman and known trickster Norm Cash, just laughed his buttocks off at my misery. I didn't much care for him after that... or for Chaw either!

Aside from such pranks, some days strange things would happen on the field and you would need to improvise... sometimes, brief moments of fame would come as a result.

One night in July, late in a tight game against the Yankees, a base runner slid into second so hard that it popped the base out of its socket, having come to rest a couple feet away. Well, the umpire went over and fooled with it for a while. A couple of players joined in, but to no avail.

About then, one of the Bench Coaches grabbed a cleat cleaning tool, tossed it to me and said "Go fix it kid!" So, there I was streaming to second base with every intention of handing the tool to the ump or one of the players for them to reattach the base, but nope. They all just looked at each other, then at me and said "Fix it kid."

Well, I really had no experience with mounting bases, but I dug around for a minute, saw the problem and easily slipped the base back into its sleeve. Relieved, the ump and players all shook my hand and as I ran back to my post the fans gave me a standing ovation.

Sharkey later said to me "hmmm, ummm, heard you done something good out there tonight for a change." With nothing more to say, he simply turned and walked away. You know, it just doesn't get any better than that!

*　　　*　　　*

So, now the game is over and the Day is coming to an end... well, not really. All that equipment now had to get back into the Clubhouse. God forbid it rained that day because we would also then need to clean it all up first if it had.

Once back in the Clubhouse, the three of us got to tackle the "best" part of this job... our favorite task... cleaning and polishing about 35 to 40 pairs of shoes, or about 12 to 15 pair each. Yup, dirty, smelly and sweaty leather cleats… Yum! As I mentioned earlier, players were really particular about their shoes and we got very good at tending to them.

Typical 1965 Baseball Cleats… Ready for Cleaning and Polishing!

Now don't get the impression that the Boys of Summer back then were more focused on their personal appearance than the players of today. Nope, that was not the reason why they were so particular about their shoes. Truthfully, the guys back then loved to get just as dirty playing the Game as the players do in our current era. Nope, one thing I learned for sure during *My Year* was that everything in baseball happens for a reason and a purpose. And behind those reasons, there is almost always a story.

So in this case, the shoe polishing obsession came about due to the events surrounding an otherwise obscure player named Vernal "Nippy" Jones. It was the 1957 World Series, Game 4, between the New York Yankees and the Milwaukee Braves. The Yanks were leading the Series two games to one at the time.

New York Yankee great Elston Howard had just tied the game in the top of the ninth inning with two outs and two runners on base. Howard shocked the home team crowd by cracking a three-run blast to deep left field.

In the top of the tenth inning the Yankees scored again. Now with the Braves behind by one run in the bottom-half of tenth inning, 5-4, Jones came in to lead-off the frame, pinch-hitting for future Hall of Fame pitching star Warren Span.

A low pitch neared Jones, slightly grazing him in the foot. However, the Home Plate Umpire, Augie Donatelli called it a ball, apparently not seeing the infraction as his *uniform coattails* of that era blocked his view. Jones respectfully protested, insisting that the baseball had indeed hit his foot. He politely asked Augie to check the ball and sure enough, a mark of shoe polish now adorned it.

Nippy was awarded first base to the utter dismay of famed Yankees' Manager, Casey Stengel who was never afraid to protest a call. He lost that one though; the ball was marked and Jones stood tall at first base, nobody out.

The Braves went on to score three runs in the tenth to win the game 7-5 on an Eddie Matthews two-run shot, evening that Series at two games apiece. The "Shoeshine Incident" as it would later be called, was the turning point in the Series, as the Braves then went on to win the 1957 World Series in seven games.

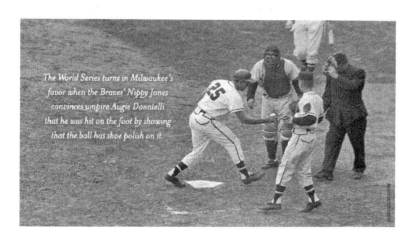

The World Series turns in Milwaukee's favor when the Braves' Nippy Jones convinces umpire Augie Donatelli that he was hit on the foot by showing that the ball has shoe polish on it.

A smudge of Shoe Polish on the Ball Proved
that Jones Had Been Hit by a Pitch!

Here's what Hall of Famer and Braves Player Hank Aaron later had to say about Nippy's unusual feat.

> *"At that point (in the 1957 World Series), we were in imminent danger of going down three games to one, and I don't think anybody in America would have imagined that the guy who would turn the Series around would be Nippy Jones.*
> *Nippy was a first baseman who had been out of the big leagues for five years before we brought him up to fill in when Adcock was hurt, and he had never really made his mark—until this day. When he did, the mark was on his shoe."*
> *Courtesy, Hank Aaron in "I Had a Hammer: The Hank Aaron Story," 1992*

Years later, a similar incident happened to another Jones, Cleon Jones of the Miracle Mets, to be exact. It was the 1969 World Series between the New York Mets and the Baltimore Orioles. Just one more little factoid in the long list of winning miracles for the 1969 World Series Champs, those Amazing Mets!

Baseball shoes soon would no longer be made of leather as many players opted for the new stylized brands such as Nike and Adidas… polish optional. Now available in all types of team and neon colors, I wonder what the Bat Boys of today do after their games!

Well back then, the three of us sure took our polishing seriously and if not, we always had Sharkey to critique our work. So, had events fallen differently for me in my life, I could have easily made it as a shoe-shine guy working at a large hotel or at an airport someplace. In fact, I can still put a shine on some good leather that might blind your eyes if the light hits it just right. As I have learned, it's always good to have a Plan B in life!

*   *   *

Back in the Clubhouse, if the Visiting Team lost, we might need to lay low for a while until a hot-headed player or two vented their, um, disappointment with the game. This only became even more exciting if the manager decided to have one of the players come by his office for a lively chat about their performance that night. Not for the faint of heart! And back then, reporters did not have access to the Clubhouse immediately after games… sometimes that made for some mighty spicy conversations before they were let in to do their interviews.

So with all the players having now gone back to their hotel and with our own work completed, it was now time for us to go home… showers optional, ready to do it all over again the next day. Just another day at the 'ol ballpark for some pretty tired young fellas!

You might be wondering at this point, since a good portion of the Major League season takes place while school was still in session, how did we handle our school responsibilities and obligations and still do our Bat Boy jobs? Luckily, the White Sox played most of their weekday games at night. That allowed for me to be able to go to school until mid-afternoon and then make the mad twenty-five mile dash to Comiskey Park in rush hour traffic while still arriving at the field a couple of hours before game time.

Clearly, this was a demanding schedule, but somehow my cohorts and I still found some time to complete our homework on most days. Well, mostly. I mean really, would you force your fourteen year old kid to stay up all night to complete a lousy term paper when he had just cleaned the slime and goo off of 15 pairs of Major League cleats after an already exhausting eighteen hour day? Ah, the glamour of it all!

See, there were even times when the grain ran true in the 1965 Chicago White Sox Visiting Team Bat Boy Crew.

Some of the Many Looks I Had as the White Sox Visiting Team Bat Boy

A VERY SPECIAL DAY

After a short time on the job, the Visiting Team Crew and I had pretty well learned the ropes of our various Bat Boy roles around Comiskey Park. The same was true on the Home Team side as Fred and his guys settled into their routines as well.

Still, every now and then something unique would happen that would remind us all of just how special that summer was and how fortunate we were to be in the positions we were. One such day stands out above all others and it was made possible by the complete generosity of the Chicago White Sox.

About mid-season, we were all asked to get to the ballpark about an hour early one day. Once we got into our uniforms, all six of us were requested to report to the area around home plate. There, White Sox General Manager Ed Short really shocked us when he presented each of us with our very own, custom made Hillerich & Bradsby, Louisville Slugger bat.

In my case, it was that Genuine *Davis* Louisville Slugger pictured earlier. It was the same style (model K48) used by many great players such as Carl Yastrzemski and later, by Rickey Henderson. It was a beautiful piece of lumber and it fit me just right.

Adding to the ceremonial aspect of the event, many of the Sox players came out to help make this day even more special. Leading the way that afternoon were third baseman, Pete Ward, centerfielder, Ken Berry and catcher, Johnny Romano… three of the finest young men one could ever hope to meet. Oh, yes, the grain ran quite true in those men.

Pete Ward, Ken Berry, Johnny Romano & My Sister Cheryl

After a moment or two, Pete was the first to say "Now that you've got some new wood, we got to try 'em out!" With that, Romano got in his squat behind the plate, Pete toed the rubber on the mound and the other White Sox players went out to various positions around the field.

While Ward was not a Major League pitcher, as a third baseman he did have a gun for an arm... after all, he was the 1963 American League Co-Rookie of the Year! I don't recall who his first "casualty" was that day, but about three or four other kids took their chances to swing (and mostly miss) at fast balls coming from a Big Leaguer. As with me, most of the Contest kids played Little and/or Pony League ball, but Pete's 85 mile per hour plus heater was something we had never seen while in a batter's box. Up until then, the best any of us had seen with a stick in our hands was about 70 miles per hour... big difference!

Everybody on the field was having a good time and enjoying the laughs, but then out of the bullpen came a large, looming figure headed toward the mound... and it was now my turn to bat. Well, this fellow, who will remain nameless out of courtesy, was a fire-balling Latino Lefty and he was now toeing the rubber and glaring in at me.

I was told later that this very accomplished pitcher, who was having a rough year due to some nagging injuries, wanted to get some work in off the field mound. Because I was physically as big, or even bigger than most of the players, he chose me to be his prey.

In addition to never having seen a 90 mile per hour plus fastball, I also had very little history facing a Lefty. In any case, there I was, shaking in my shoes.

I looked at pitch one. It came and went before I could blink my eyes. I figured my best bet would be to try to bunt the next pitch, but afterward the Lefty stared at me and yelled something off-color in Spanish… luckily, I didn't speak much Spanish then!

Not clear as to why, I repeated my bunt attempt on pitch number three. Seems, that didn't go over too well either with that imposing figure on the bump. Now, he was shouting something even more unpleasant sounding in Spanish and flailing his arms at me.

Confused, I looked back at Johnny and asked him what was up with all that commotion. He said, "What do you think you are doing kid?" I said, I was just trying to time the pitch like my Dad had taught me to do.

He looked up at me through his catcher's mask and said "What, are you nuts? If you touch a ball with your bat that guy out there on the mound will probably come over here and break your neck! So just take your swings, sit down and someday you will be able to tell your kids that you once got to bat against a top-level Major Leaguer pitcher."

Okidoki, now I got it. I guess ol' Mr. Lefty didn't see this as a good time for Bob the Bat Boy to shine at the ballpark! Pitch four was now on its way… and now… it was on its way back to him from Romano! Seems my swing was just a tad late. Pitch five… at least this time I got to see Johnny throwing the ball back to the Big Lefty.

Now, fully determined to see what I could actually do with my new lumber and in complete defiance of Romano's advice I suppose, I decided to change my tactics. This time I would start my swing just as Mr. Lefty completed his wind-up. Then, at the top of his delivery and while he was about to drop his stride leg forward, I saw the ball poised in the grip of his hand.

In the blink of an eye, that rocket was now released and screaming toward the inner third of the plate, thigh-high. Accelerating my hands and swinging as hard as I could... WHACK! Yes, my new Louisville Slugger connected squarely with that ball, launching it 370 feet to the left field Power Ally and into the front row seats. "What a sight!" I thought. That was until I caught something out of the corner of my eye rushing towards me from the mound.

For the first time in my life I actually saw what looked like steam coming off a human being. His nose was snorting with anger and his eyes were now as wide as the baseball I had just hit. The look of a wounded predator filled my thoughts as he was charging Home Plate like a tormented bull. Meanwhile, the other ball players, in utter disbelief, were rolling around the ground in hysterics, laughing their respective bottoms off... had a Bat Boy just taken Mr. Big Shot Yard?

Well, I was never a fast runner, but that afternoon I bet I could have beaten Jesse Owens in the 100 yard dash! Off, I took down the first base line for the open space of the outfield with the infuriated Bull seeing red and in hot pursuit. Finally, some of the other players stepped in and tried to calm him down a bit.

Romano helped the most, telling his battery mate that, "It really wasn't the kid's fault... he closed his eyes and the bat just happened to hit the ball... one in a million shot... your stuff looked great today. I bet you'll be back on the hill real soon!"

Naturally, I was just fine with that story and Mr. Lefty departed the field, still swearing profusely in Spanish. I retreated to the relative safety of the Visiting Dugout and up the tunnel, never knowing if the last kid got his chance to hit that day or not.

Thinking that I might be in some kind of trouble, I kept that experience to myself for a couple days. Then someone mentioned what had happened to my Dad and he then asked me about it. I hemmed and hawed a bit, but then sheepishly said "Yes" that I had done it. My Dad just smiled.

Luckily for me, I didn't see Mr. Lefty very often for the rest of the season. However, when I did, that nasty, all too familiar scowl reappeared on his face. I guess some guys just can't see the humor in such things!

*   *   *

Truthfully, smacking that ball felt really good and it helped make-up for one of the saddest experiences I ever had growing-up. And it all had to do with my Dad and baseball. Let me explain.

My Dad was a volunteer coach for our local Pony League for many years. Strangely though, my Dad was never *my* coach. In fact, the teams I was on competed against his. I was never sure why he wanted it that way, but I guess he didn't want me to feel pressured to play just because of his love of the Game. Who knows?

I wish he had realized that I played because I loved the Game too and I would have cherished being on his team. Being a dad is a complex thing and all we can do is hope that we did the best we knew how to at the time. The rest is in God's hands.

Now with that bit of background, here's the story. 1964, the year before my becoming the Bat Boy, was my last year in Pony League Baseball (**P**rotect **O**ur **N**ation's **Y**outh.) Back then, there were no elite travel teams like today, so Pony was the highest level of play around for most 7th and 8th graders.

Current Day Emblem Representing the Pony League World Series.

I was a pretty decent player and an 8th grader. Even by then, I was already a big kid and usually batted clean-up on my regular team. Thus, when it became time for kids to be picked for the annual All-Star team, I was pretty psyched.

Normally our little town never did too well in those competitions, usually getting knocked-out in the first round by our rival and big jock-town, Northbrook. But in those days, competing in the Pony League World Series was kind of a big deal. Somewhat like the Little League World Series, but for kids a little older, this tournament would conclude with its National Championship Series in California. Just the prospect of it was a dream come true for a bunch of Midwestern kids.

To get there though, teams from all over the US would battle it out, first at a local level, then regionally, followed with those winners going on to Sectionals. The winners of the four Sectionals would then travel on to the Championship round in the fantasyland known to us as LA.

Given our location, our Sectional was to be held in Laramie, Wyoming... half way to LA! Kind of a big deal for kids from

Illinois, really. And for the first time in years, our town had some very talented kids ready to play ball. Kids like Buzz Avery, Tommy Mickalic and the Mauer brothers to name a few... in 1964, those kids could play!

The way the All-Star team selection process worked was that the coaches from the regular season teams would meet as a group with the League President. They would then select fifteen players to the main Roster, with two additional kids chosen as Alternates in case any of the Roster kids couldn't play for some reason along the way.

1965 White Sox Ace, Joe Horlen Once Played in the Pony League World Series. In Fact, He is the Only Baseball Player to Play on Teams that Won a Pony League World Series (1952), a College World Series (Oklahoma State-1959), and a Major League World Series (Oakland Athletics-1972.)

My excitement really heightened when I learned a few days before the meeting that my Dad was chosen to be the Assistant Coach for the All-Star team, since his regular season team was then in second place in the League. Mr. Smith's (not his real name) team was in first place, so he got the Head Coaching spot.

Then one Wednesday evening at about 7 PM, all the coaches gathered at our local Park District Office and I waited at home, excitedly looking forward to my Dad's triumphant return. You see, it was pretty well accepted that the All-Star Coach's kids were automatically selected for the Team. The remaining spots were then voted on by the coaches, who in most cases would take their own kid as a first pick, leaving the remaining spots to be voted on by the committee. In many cases, those coaches kids were among the best players in the League anyway, so that was acceptable to most everyone.

Unfortunately, Mr. Smith's kid was, well let's just say, not an ideal ballplayer. In fact, he was so bad and athletically limited that no one expected that he would get on the team, even with his dad as the Head Coach. Seems that this situation would uncover a flaw in the system that delayed the proceedings a bit.

All that night I paced around our house waiting to hear the good news. Time was dragging for sure. By now it was after 10 PM, CDT and still no Dad. I watched the late News and Weather on WLS and then a bit of the Tonight Show with Johnny Carson on WMAQ. By 11:00 PM, I was really getting worried, but I needed to get ready for bed. So up the stairs I went to my room, stopping to brush my teeth before slipping into bed, too wired to sleep.

About a half hour later, I heard the door from the garage open. I got a waft of smoke from Dad's ever-present cigar as it preceded him up the stairs to my room while he made his usual cup of late evening tea in the kitchen.

Well, the rest of the story was reported to me by my Dad. To be fair, my Dad always prided himself on being an honorable man of high moral principles. He had served as a Deacon in our

Community Church and had been an airplane pilot in the Navy during World War II. As the Commander of his crew, he would often rise to being the voice of reason when disputes arose on-board the big super-charged, multi-engine airplanes he flew to help save the World. He was also known as a really nice guy by most everyone. Sometimes to a fault.

All of a sudden there he was, standing before me with a big grin on his face. My heart pounding, he told me that it had been a quite a night for him and the other coaches. He went on to tell me that the League President started the proceedings by suggesting that the custom of having the two All-Star Coaches' kids be the first picks of the night be continued.

"Immediately" Dad said, "an objection came from several of the other coaches." It seemed that those guys figured we had a pretty good crop of kids that could compete well in the 1964 Series. To increase our competitiveness by fielding the best possible team, Dad said that those guys suggested that Mr. Smith's son, Alvin be designated as the Honorary, First Alternate of the team, for all the obvious reasons. "That would have left you as the first Roster pick" Dad said.

"However" he continued, "Mr. Smith was none too keen on that idea"… so much so that he told the group that "if my kid isn't on the main Roster, then I am out as the Head Coach."

Not wanting such a rift in the ranks, the President intervened and said "OK, there you have it then. Smith and Davis' kids are in, let's get on with it." My Dad could have left it at that and I would have been on the Roster, but then again… I guess he just couldn't.

With a look of great pride in his eyes he told me that he then addressed the group. He told them that "Only the best players should be picked for the team, irrespective of the coach's relationship to the kid." After all, he said, "This is to be an *All-Star* team and only the most deserving players should be selected." Quite a speech!

But, as you can imagine, the group didn't like his idea any more than Mr. Smith had liked their idea about his kid's role on the team earlier. After all, they each sure as heck wanted their own kid on the team and my Dad's suggestion would put that in jeopardy. Long moments of silence followed, he said.

Then, in his ultimate act of self-righteousness, my Dad told the group that "Well OK, do what you will, but I remove Bob from the automatic roster selection. If you guys vote him in at the end, then he's in. Otherwise, he can be an Alternate."

As he told me this, this odd look of realization began to cover his face as he saw me staring at him in obvious disbelief. In fact, I couldn't believe my ears... "he must be joking" I thought to myself. But no, it was true. My own Dad had thrown me off the All-Star team, and just for some false sense of propriety it seemed to me.

After those words from my Dad, it only made sense that none of the other coaches would intervene and vote me in. Heck, if my own Dad didn't stand-up for my being on the team, who were they to do otherwise?

About then, I sensed that for some reason Dad seemed kind of angry **at them** for remaining mute about me as all the other kids got picked. How could he be surprised at **their** actions when it is **he** that squashed my All-Star dreams?

After that, I told him that I needed to get to sleep. I rolled over in my bed and pulled up the covers and he left, cigar smoke lingering in the humid summer night air. However, I never did attain REM sleep that night, I can assure you.

Few times in my life have I ever tossed and turned so much in an effort to find the solitude of sleep. No, my Dad's words kept replaying in my head, me in disbelief... my heart bleeding.

Yup, with that brief but misguided speech by my Dad, I was relegated to being an Alternate on what became the best Pony League All-Star Team to ever come from my hometown.

In fact, they not only beat Northbrook, but also defeated a highly ranked team from Maywood, IL, a powerhouse team from Paducah, KY and our toughest opponent, the boys from Hamtramck, MI to capture the Regional's. Quite a run!

Now *they*, the All-Stars from Glenview, IL were on *their* way to Wyoming. And like a little lost kid, I had to endure every mile of that five day journey with them. No, not as a member of the team, but just as the "Not good enough" son of a Coach.

Believe it or not, for most of that trip I was left to sit alone, no longer one of the guys. Meanwhile, my Mom sat proudly by my Dad's side as that big bus headed west.

As you might expect, little "Albee" Smith as we called him, started at second base in most *every* game they played in that tournament. As predicted, he racked-up a multitude of errors while producing no hits in all those Local and Regional games. Hmmm.

In the end, it was his critical error that helped end that great team's run, one sunny day in Wyoming. He did beat-out one infield hit on a bunt though, so hats off to him, 1-37.

But as bad as Albee was, at least he would always have some great memories from that experience. Even if in his heart he knew that he didn't deserve to be on that team based on his own merits, he probably never questioned that *his* dad would always look out for him and promote him when his position allowed. Forlorn, I had no such feelings.

Now you might say, "What's the big deal, at least you were still on the team." Well, I was not on that team in any real practical sense. No uniform or even a team cap was issued to Alternates. Alternates could not even practice with the team and they were never welcomed in the dugout, except to carry out the equipment and leftover trash after the game. Heartbreaking for a thirteen year old baseball lover.

No trophies, no name in the paper, no nothing. The other Alternate had bailed after the game in Northbrook, the embarrassment, peer pressure and frustration too great. Me, I just cried to myself... all the while watching the other kids playing the Game, with my Dad leading the way. In all honesty, few things in my life have ever stung me so deeply.

As I later learned, a team from Long Beach, CA won the National Championship that year. Can't say I had much of a problem with that... no offense to the 1964 Pony League Team from Glenview, IL. By then, I just had no more cheers in me.

Yes, the grain ran true in my Dad, and I loved him and his well-intentioned ways. Perhaps, I rationalized, "Maybe Dad just made up that story to save my feelings. Maybe I was never going to be on the Roster at all, coach's kid or not. Maybe I just wasn't good enough to make the team on my own merits after all." The doubt was agonizing.

Eventually though, I realized that his story was true… I mean really, there was no way on Earth that little Albee would have otherwise been voted on to that team. And even more painfully, some of the other kids got the same story from their coach dads, which they in turn were only too happy to share with me in tortuous detail. My Dad, the good man that he was, in his heroic effort to bring righteousness to that panel of coaches, kind of made fools out of both of us that summer night in July. Some pills are painfully bitter to swallow.

To be clear, I wanted to make that team on my own merits first and foremost. But in the end, I just really wanted to be on the team. I felt I was good enough to make it on my own, but I sure didn't need my Dad of all people taking it away from me.

Truthfully, I am not at all sure why my Dad did what he did. I will say that I never got the sense that he had any remorse over it as I think he truly believed that what he did was a good thing. We never talked about it after that night in my bedroom. Kinda wish we had, but stuff like that just wasn't in him I guess.

In hindsight, I believe that it really wasn't very *nice* of Mr. Smith to use his positional power and stated threat to advance his kid onto a team that he no more belonged on than the Man in the Moon. That having been said, by previous custom it was *permissible* that he got Albee on the team, even if it wasn't popular or even *fair*. I bet Albee had no trouble falling to sleep that night after his dad got home and told him that *he* had made the team. The "how of it" details likely left out… In the end, "Daddy Ball" would live on.

On the positive side, I can assure you that I kept the memory of those events foremost in my thoughts as I later embarked into parenthood myself. Sure, I am certain that I screwed-up my parenting in many ways, but I can honestly say that I doubt that my kids ever questioned my devotion to their endeavors… maybe to a fault in the other direction… who knows. However, as I said before, being a dad is not an easy thing. So keep your eyes open to see what my kids might have to say about the job I did, if they ever write their own books someday! ☺

As if to prove the point, over the next year I got firm evidence that God does often work in unexpected and mysterious ways. Yes, 1964 would soon pass and a new year would blossom. And with my Dad's help, 1965 would become *My Year.*

*   *   *

One last story about my bat, and a little more about its importance to me. For fear of breaking it, the last time I used *My* Louisville Slugger was in a Colt League game later that summer in *My Year.* Given my time commitments to the White Sox, I didn't get the opportunity to attend those games very often, so getting to play the Game was a real treat.

Then, for the first time in months, around the fifth inning, the coach had me pinch hit against the top high school pitcher in our area, a tough right hander known for his blazing fastball. "Yeah, Right" I thought. "Bet he can't bring it as fast as the Big Lefty did." I was correct.

Because I was known for being a decent fastball hitter, Mr. High School started me off with something off-speed, which I anticipated and took for a ball. "And now for the heater" I thought.

Guess what? Thigh-high, inner third of the plate, just like what ol' Mr. Lefty had sent my way. Bam… 400 feet to straight away center! Oh, and this time, my Dad was there to see me do it.

Yes, that day in the summer of 1965 when that piece of prized lumber was gifted to me by the Chicago White Sox, well, that was a good day for me… Yes, A Very Special Day indeed!

*Al Lopez (center) Celebrates a New Sox Managerial Contract
with GM Ed Short (left) and Sox Owner Arthur Allyn (right).
Those Men Made 1965, My Year, Very Special Indeed!*

SOME LESSONS ARE
TAUGHT THE HARD WAY

My hometown, Glenview, Illinois was a great place to grow up. In the early days it could have been confused for a slightly overgrown *Mayberry*, of Andy Griffith fame.

Friendly and genteel people filled the local churches each Sunday and the marching bands, floats and fireworks always showed-up on the Fourth of July. Modest affluence abounded and we all could walk or ride our bikes to town for a visit to the local Dairy Queen during the warm months or to the local soda fountain at Renneckers Drug Store the rest of the year.

A nice young man took over the local barber shop and everybody learned to accept that Bob the Barber had in fact replaced the long standing previous owner (I think his name might have been Floyd ☺) who had retired to Florida.

We also had a great little league baseball venue in town and each park had grass infields and 200 foot fences. I sure learned a lot about the Game (*and* some things about human nature too) on those ball fields. Years later, they were renamed in honor of my Eighth Grade PE teacher, Mr. Dave Tosh, who remains an icon in Glenview sports history to this very day.

I even worked at the historic general store named Rugen's where you could roam from hardware, to groceries to menswear and into dry goods all under the same large roof. My brother Larry, worked in menswear, which fit him well. For me, working in that hardware store was one of most educational jobs I ever had. From that time on, I became quite the handyman around a house!

Glenview was so small that we did not even have a movie

theater in town. So, on many Saturdays my brother and I would take a public bus about eight miles to the City of Evanston to go to either the Varsity or Valencia movie theaters there. We probably started doing that when we were about eleven and eight respectively, fully with our parents' permission... can you imagine that by today's overly protective standards?

Once there, we would spend the day watching movies and eating popcorn. To us, Evanston was a "big" town and parts of it were also considered to be kind of "rough" in those days. Thus, we were always on our guard when we hopped off the bus and headed the few blocks to the theaters. In the end though, we never did encounter any troubles on any of those journeys.

All I know for sure about all that was the bus rides to and fro were usually filled with pleasant speaking black women dressed in maids uniforms heading to or from the wealthy parts of Wilmette and Glenview.

Other than Carl who ran our local Phillips 66 gas station, they were about the only black people I ever saw in our little town. Thus, my slate was clean when it came to judging racial issues... every person of color I had met was always nice to me.

My Hometown. See the Sign for Rugen's?
We Thought of Glenview as Mayberry North!

So, in addition to being in Illinois and not in North Carolina, two other things made Glenview a bit different than the mythical Mayberry. One difference was that the United States Navy had built a rather significant Air Station (NAS) there before World War II.

In fact, I would one day be brought to life as a result of my Dad meeting my Mom while he was stationed in pilot flight school there during the War. They would later marry and move to the civilian side of Glenview after the War ended. First my brother Larry arrived, a few years later I showed-up, followed some six years later by my sister Cheryl.

June 29, 1953: The NAS Glenview baseball team.
Chicago Tribune Historical Photo.

The other thing that made Glenview a bit different from Mayberry was that a commuter train ran directly through town, allowing business people to easily go back and forth to Chicago where the big-buck jobs were. And, the areas west of town were ripe for expansion. Thus, a good part of our town became quite affluent as a result, although our family was fully entrenched in the middle income bracket.

With easy access to Chicago and few obstacles impairing expansion, our small little town of 6,100 residents in the 1950s exploded to an astounding 25,000 people a few years later when it became *My Year*. Much good would come from that over time, but the initial impact was to bring with it a lack of community, continuity and intimacy for which the town had been previously known. Mayberry North was to be no more.

Nonetheless, the values and mores I learned growing up as I did prepared me well for life in many ways. However, one area that it had not prepared me for was life in the Urban Jungle, where my Bat Boy days would soon take me. Yes, there were many lessons to be learned in 1965. And in *My Year*, many of those had nothing to do with baseball.

Now, the work of getting me to work was underway. My pristine little village stood in complete contrast to the areas surrounding, and en route to White Sox Park. Getting to the ballpark, some twenty-plus miles away over their eighty-plus home game schedule did pose some real challenges.

On most days, my parents would take advantage of the free Home Season Pass I won in the Contest and go to the game. But I needed to be at the Park two and a half hours before each game. My Dad, a Chartered Life Underwriter and Insurance Broker, generally worked a normal Monday thru Friday work-week, so he couldn't take me on those days. And, it didn't really work to have my Mom drive me there early and then have to drive all the way back home to get my Dad and then make the long trek back south in time for the game to start.

Weekend games made all of that much simpler because my parents and I could then make the drive together. Thus, in an attempt to find a reasonable means of getting me to Comiskey on weekdays, we decided to see if public transportation could provide that solution. If that could work in getting me there, then I would be able to ride home with my parents after most of the games.

On those days, my Mom would pick me up early from school and drive me to the Glenview train station. I would then take a southbound commuter train into Union Station in Chicago. Then I would walk about five city blocks through the cities' Financial District to catch the Chicago Transportation Authority (CTA) Elevated Train (or "L" as it is known) which would then take me to within a mile or so of the Ballpark. Exiting the L Station, I would then head west on foot along 35th Street to the Employee Entrance at Comiskey.

1960s CTA Elevated or "L" Train.

On paper, it seemed like a decent solution. However, in reality this turned out not to be an ideal plan for two reasons.

One was, that all took about two hours to complete. More importantly though, that area between the L Station and Comiskey was in the heart of the "Projects" otherwise known as the Robert Taylor Homes. No, my Mayberry-like upbringing had not well-prepared me for the danger lurking on that harrowing journey. And no, back then, a lily-white, fourteen year old suburban kid strolling along those streets was not a common sight to see. But for a while, the plan worked, even though I was scared to death the whole way when I took that walk.

When I finally reached the Dan Ryan Expressway, the Employee Entrance to the Ballpark was in view and just a few blocks further. Only then would I begin to breathe a bit easier. However, that would soon prove to be no safe harbor either.

By all accounts, this attempt at providing quality housing to Chicago's poor failed miserably. After years of crime, drugs, extreme gang warfare and general dismay, these hell-holes were subsequently torn down, along with the infamous Cabrini Green Complex on the near North Side of the City that suffered from the same ills. I am glad to say that the area around US Cellular Field (which replaced Comiskey) has improved greatly since that time.

The Robert Taylor Homes Housing Project in 1962.

Originally designed to house 11,000 residents, it peaked at 27,000, with 95% of those people on public assistance. The Project produced one of the highest crime rate areas in the United States. In fact, in one weekend, more than 300 separate shooting incidents, with 28 deaths were reported there. Not the best place for a hike to Comiskey.

However, long before all of that was to happen, on this one Saturday in early June, 1965, the Sox had a day game. As it turned out, on that particular day my parents were going to attend a wedding and therefore would not be attending the game. Accordingly, I needed to find my way to *and* from Comiskey that day via the above route... a chilling thought indeed.

That morning, I made it to the Park without incident. The game went by quickly and I even scored a broken bat to boot! Given the foreboding journey I had laying ahead, I decided not to carry that piece of lumber home with me that night... that decision would become fortuitous.

The Crew and I finished our chores and by now it was late afternoon and the sun hung brightly, shining from the west. As I left the Park, the surrounding area in all directions was deserted. Unlike the Cubs home, Wrigley Field on the North side where parties in the neighborhood establishments continued non-stop before, during and after games, there were no such attractions to keep folks around White Sox Park before or after a game. Nope, all that lay before me was frightening.

*A Stroll Through the Robert Taylor Homes in
1965 Was Not for the Faint of Heart.*

With no other choice available to me on that day, I
reluctantly headed on my reverse journey to the L Station. As I
began crossing the Dan Ryan on 35th Street, I noticed a group
of local youths heading my way from across the overpass. I
guess I could have turned around, but there really was no place
to go as the Employee Entrance to the Park was now locked
behind me.

There were about twelve of them, ranging from just little kids
to a couple taller than me. As we neared, I stepped off the
raised sidewalk and onto the street to let them pass. I later
learned that was a miscalculation as it was taken as a sign of
weakness on my part... and honestly, I have to say that I **was**
feeling a bit weak at that point.

So as we met, I saw that several of the kids were holding
knives and devices known as zip guns... Uh Oh. I kept looking
ahead, but one of the really tall kids spoke. All he said was "Hey

man, you gotta dime?" As I turned to reply, the low hanging sun blinded my eyes. At that very second I felt a blow to my left jaw. Stunned, I dropped to one knee. Meanwhile, the little kids jumped on me and started pounding furiously on my head and back with their fists for a brief moment. Coming back to my senses, I quickly rose, tossing those kids off me as I began to run toward the L Station as fast as I could.

As I scurried to my escape, I saw that two of those little kids almost fell over the guard rail and on to the busy Expressway, some thirty five feet below. I kept running and then turned briefly again to see that they had been saved from falling. Meanwhile, the bigger ones were just standing there and laughing... I didn't really see the humor in the whole thing so I just kept on sprinting to the station as fast as I could. Fear can be an extremely powerful emotion and in my terrorized state that day, I think I probably set a new world record for the one mile dash.

I boarded the L, at the correct Station, but I was still really shook-up. Sure, I had had a few friendly fights with school kids I knew before, but this was different... way different and fear gripped me to my core.

As it turned out, I was so racked with fear that I missed my stop for Union Station, making matters only worse. I then found myself in no man's land at the end of the L line without a clue of what to do. I finally found a pay phone and placed a collect call home. No cell phones, remember?

Thankfully, my brother Larry was there and he told me to transfer to the adjacent Skokie Swift Train that ended a mere five miles from my home. Moments later as I exited that rattling old train car, I saw him rushing towards me in his prized 1957 Ford Fairlane Convertible to complete my rescue. At long last, I finally could take a deep breath.

The Skokie Swift, With Its Overhead Power lines Was the End of the North Bound Line in the 1960s.

By the time my parents returned home that night from the wedding, I was having a rough go of it. The fear of what could have happened to me that afternoon had overwhelmed me; I simply had to cry and vomit it all out of my system. I cannot even begin to imagine how awful my parents must have felt seeing me like that. In the end, their presence provided the comfort I needed to sleep soundly through the night.

I have faced a lot in my life and if it had not been for this experience, I may not have made it through some of them. Yes, I learned a lot that day about fear... but there was still more to learn from that experience.

My Dad called White Sox Security the next morning to tell them what had happened, but there really wasn't anything that they could do. Word then began to spread through the Clubhouse and people (even Sharkey) expressed their empathy for what had happened as I returned to my duties that Sunday.

Our Ball Boy, Greg lived somewhere around 79th and Halsted Streets, which was quite a distance south from Comiskey and the Projects. Like most kids in his neighborhood, he was by no means a gang member. But he was a black kid from another part of town and those young thugs who assaulted me would have assumed that he was from a rival gang because in their minds *every* black kid belonged to a gang. After all, **they** all did; as did most every male over six years of age that lived in the Robert Taylor Homes at that time. That was just the law of the Urban Jungle. Greg's words to me that morning have always stuck with me. He simply said "Sorry what happened, but you were lucky. If it had been me, I'd be dead."

As I would learn, under almost any scenario that hostile group of young thugs would have treated Greg, a fellow black youth, in a much different fashion than they had me. Yes, Greg would have been toast. A miscalculation such as the one I had made could have cost him much more than a bit of fear and anguish. Heck, he had to deal with *those* emotions every time he ventured too far away from his home "hood."

It was then that I began to realize that I knew nothing about life in *that* world. As I would learn, I was just a passing amusement to those gang-bangers… I posed no turf threat, no physical threat, no threat at all. In fact, I was just "practice" for those kids.

However, it was lucky that I had not brought my newly acquired bat with me that afternoon as that could have significantly changed those dynamics. Yes, as Greg confirmed, that bat would have either been stolen from me, used to assault me further or used by me in a futile attempt to protect myself. In any case, it was good that it stood safely in my locker in the White Sox Visitors Clubhouse where I had left it.

I learned a lot in those two days and I am better for it… I just wonder though, will this craziness ever cease? Even after all these years and all the things that have been done to change those dynamics, much of them haven't. Just one more failed "Project" after another. Just another day of gangbanging attacks on each other and on the defenseless. What a tragic way to have to grow up.

Many days and nights Greg took CTA buses from his home to the Park and back again. On each such journey he faced the dangers I encountered that day… just with the possibility of far worse results. Greg Driskell, he indeed was a very brave young man.

*   *   *

Now a new plan was needed to get me to the Park. A couple nights later, my Dad received a telephone call from Fred's father. Mr. Croft said that he had heard about what had happened and wondered if they could help.

Since the Croft's lived just a few miles from us in the adjacent suburb of Wilmette, Mr. Croft suggested that perhaps Fred could pick me up before the games and then we could share the ride the rest of the way to the Park… sharing the cost as well of course. So far, so good. Then the zinger.

For a mere $2.00, Fred would come the *four* miles out of his way from his house in his 1960 VW Bug and pick me up. We would then go together the extra *four* miles it took to get back to the entrance of the Eden's Expressway from where he had come. Then we would complete the drive south to the Comiskey together. And, the Blue Light Special of the Day was that they would only charge *$3.00* for round trips… such a deal! And to seal the deal, Fred's dad reportedly reiterated that we should not forget that there was safety in numbers.

Safety perhaps… rip-off for sure. It had previously been costing me $0.55 to take public transportation to the Park ($0.30 for the commuter train into Chicago and another $0.25 for the L ride to the 35th Street Station.) We got paid $6 in wages for a whole game and this "cab fare" was going to take one third of that for going *EIGHT* miles, or about *ten minutes* out of this "Cabbies" way… Hmmm. As the well-known television icon Judge Judy might say, "Reeeediculous, Absolutely Ridiculous Sir!"

Not to chew on sour grapes, but I had always wondered how

Mr. Croft could morally justify taking such advantage of this situation. Let me explain.

That 1960, forty horsepower VW Bug got around 30 miles to a gallon of gas. With its more than ten gallon fuel tank capacity, it therefore had a range of more than ***300 miles***. Thus, it could have made that trip to the Park about ***thirteen times*** on just one tank of gas. Back then, a full tank of gas would have cost between $2.80 to $3.10 depending on where one bought it. Fred was already traveling twenty miles each way to get to Comiskey, so why would a mere eight miles and ten minutes of time necessitate such a premium? Hmmm.

I also wondered why my Dad didn't demand a more equitable deal… I guess that just wasn't in him. Like I said before, sometimes he was just too nice a guy. In the end, I just do not know. What I do know is that it did put a bit of a tarnish on things with Fred.

Clearly, the arrangement with Mr. Croft wasn't directly Fred's fault, but as you can imagine, it did make for some uncomfortable commutes to the Park going forward. As it was, I had no other reasonable choice to get to Comiskey for many games. So, with a different kind of "gun" put to my head, saving for *my* college fund would just have to suffer while Fred's would prosper. Reeeediculous, Sir. Do you hear me? Ridiculous!

It was to be that in *My Year* some lessons would be taught in unexpected and sometimes, even difficult ways. The experiences I had getting to and from Comiskey that year proved to be among them. But that did not mare that fabulous season too greatly. No, being the Visiting Bat Boy for the Chicago White Sox was one of the best experiences of my life and those lessons only better prepared me for the world out of Mayberry, oh, I mean Glenview!

By my recollection, Fred was a good-looking, bright and up-beat kid. He clearly deserved to take First Place in the Contest and at age sixteen, his extra year of poise and polish was probably the deciding factor with the judges. However, to me, he often exhibited a bit higher opinion of himself than was always necessary. Maybe that is why his dad figured he deserved to earn all that bonus "Cab Fare."

I will leave the rest of those tales to him to tell when he writes his book. But let's just say that on our last ride home of the season, I stiffed him that last $3.00. And I have never regretted it for a minute!

1960s Era VW Beetle.

With 40 Horsepower it got 30 miles per gallon. It was so economical, it did not even have a fuel gauge on the interior dashboard. Luckily, it did have a Reserve Switch that provided an additional gallon of gas for when the main tank ran dry!

THE ROAD TRIP

By far, one of the greatest gifts the White Sox provided the two of us Bat Boys was a nine-day, three city, Road Trip with the team. Just imagine the thrill of being a kid, traveling in style with your favorite ball club. The memories of those days are among the best of my life. It all began with boarding the White Sox private airliner at Midway Airport on the south side of Chicago.

White Sox batboys Bob Davis and Fred Croft departed with the club Tuesday for a nine-day road trip that starts in New York and goes on to Detroit and Cleveland. The batboys were chosen in The Daily News' annual contest. From left as they boarded at Midway Airport, are first baseman Moose Skowron, Davis, third baseman Pete Ward and Croft. Sox play Yankees Wednesday night.

What a Ride!

Well, if you are going to take your first-ever airplane ride, why not do it in a private airliner surrounded by some of the best athletes in the world? And what better destination than the

95

Big Apple? And to top that off, why not take it all in on your fifteenth birthday! That was the case for me and what an adventure it was!

During our road trip, both Fred and I were treated just like the players. We shared well-furnished rooms in first class hotels in each city and received $12.00 each per day in meal money, handed to us in little Manila envelopes, just like the players. Additionally, we traveled to and from the ball fields in luxury motor coaches with the team. Whoa, this certainly was a big deal for a pair of North Suburban Chicago kids!

On our first full day in New York, we had a night game scheduled, so that gave us a good part of the day to sight-see in Manhattan. First, we saw The Empire State Building on West 34th Avenue, followed by a subway train ride to 59th Street and to the incredible Plaza Hotel in Central Park. Then we were off to the monolithic Rockefeller Center and St. Peter's Cathedral directly across the street on Fifth Avenue. We then finished the day with a trek back down to Battery Park, catching a boat ride over to the Statue of Liberty... amazing... and it only got better!

By the Way, I Was Taller than Mickey and Moose, so the Photographer Changed the Camera Angle to Make Them Look Taller... Can't have a Bat Boy Looking Down on Super Stars!

After scrambling back to the hotel, showering and getting into a change of clothes, Fred and I both met in the lobby with the team, readying ourselves for our motor coach ride to deliver us to Yankee Stadium. Our coach left the hotel in midtown, heading northward on FDR Drive along the East River, eventually crossing one of the numerous bridges into the Bronx. The coach pulled directly in front of Yankee Stadium Visitor's Entrance at about 4:30 PM.

Once inside the Clubhouse, I hurriedly dressed into my *White Sox Bat Boy uniform* and walked through the tunnel toward the dugout, hearing my baseball cleats clack on the aged pot-marked cement. As I entered the dugout, I saw the Stadium appear before me and it sent chills down my spine. This time-honored venue was overwhelming and a complete tribute to some of the greatest players in the history of the game. Yes, the Game, without doubt ran true in this Palace of Sport.

I had my Dad's old 8mm movie camera with me and I began capturing my memories in silent black and white footage. My first shots were slow, all-encompassing panoramas of the well-known gingerbread façade of the Stadium. Then, I was off to the historic Monuments. Wow, right there on the field!

"The Monuments" at Old Yankee Stadium; Right in the Field of Play.

That's Mickey Waiting for His Turn at Baseball Immortality.

Artist Rendering of the New Yankee Stadium.

Well, that old 8mm got quite a workout on that visit to New York. Many years later, we had the rolls of film I shot transferred to video tape, but the grainy quality and lack of sound made it mostly suitable for family viewing. However, the disappointing results did inspire me to later video tape my own kids every chance I could to provide lasting memories that their own kids might one day watch.

The first game of the two game set against the Yankees started on time that evening at 7:02 PM. There were slightly over twenty thousand patrons in attendance, and the weather was quite comfortable, cooling off somewhat from what had been an 80 degree day.

The best part for me was when my New Jersey relatives arrived at the Stadium in time to watch me shagging batting practice baseballs out in left field. My Dad's brother, Uncle Joe and my teen aged cousins were all there, along with a few of their friends… what a treat for all of us!

On the mound that night were two left-handed throwers; Al Downing for the Yankees, and Tommy John for the White Sox… neither pitcher would go the distance. The White Sox were in fourth place at that time, four games behind the American League leading Minnesota Twins. New York was in sixth place, twelve and one-half games behind.

Given that record, it was going to be a quiet October for the Yankees this fall, after winning five consecutive American League titles from 1960-1964. However tonight was going to be a heartbreaker for the White Sox.

The Sox were leading after six innings, 6-4, but the Yankees would tie the game in the bottom of the ninth with a two-run shot by first baseman Joe Pepitone. That was followed by a solo-blast by Tom Tresh, a career .245 hitter, in the bottom of the tenth inning. Game over!

Although the second game against the Yankees started well the next afternoon, the final results matched that of the previous night. The White Sox scored a run in the top of the first inning, but starting Yankee pitcher "Chairman of the Board," Whitey Ford, would go on to pitch a complete game, posting a 3-1 victory. The Yankees swept this short two game set. The White Sox were now on a four game skid, six and one-half games behind the league leading Minnesota Twins and hoping for better results in the coming days.

As guests of the Yankees, Fred and I would not be shining any shoes that evening as we enjoyed a quick shower just like the players. Our motor coach was parked and waiting outside the Visitor's Team Exit from the Stadium to take the team to La Guardia Airport. A game underneath the lights awaited us the next night at Tiger Stadium, 8:00 p.m., first pitch. Off to Detroit!

My first impression of Tiger Stadium was, "Boy, is this place ever green!" In fact, just about every surface in the place was painted this extremely dark green color and it was layers thick. The façades, the posts and even the seats were this forest green... made it kind of ugly to me, but it was not an uncommon treatment for those older stadiums.

And that place was *already* old in *My Year.* It was built as old stadiums of the time were with a huge playing field, but with posts and pillars that obstructed the fan's view from many seats. Still, it was an honor to walk on this hallowed ground with its giant flagpole standing proudly in the field of play out in center, about 440 feet from home plate.

When Tiger Field was finally closed following the 1999 season for the newly constructed Comerica Park, it left Fenway Park which had opened the same exact day as Tiger Stadium, April 20, 1912, as the oldest remaining baseball stadium in Major League Baseball. Wrigley Field, now the second oldest stadium was opened for the 1914 season. Dodger Stadium located at Chavez Ravine in Los Angeles, currently the third oldest ball park was built in 1962.

Tiger Stadium, 1961.

One of my more interesting stories about my time in Detroit for the four game series had almost nothing to do with baseball. It was actually an awkward situation, one that did not teach the familiar truism about the importance of being in the right place at the right time, but rather the uncomfortable consequences of being in the *wrong* place at the *wrong* time.

Our first class hotel accommodations in Detroit were located downtown, almost walking distance to Tiger Stadium situated in the old historic Corktown neighborhood. As it so happened, a church group was holding some kind of retreat for teenage girls at the same hotel.

As my luck would have it, I absentmindedly walked onto an elevator and directly into one of the girls who was on her way off the elevator. Boy, was I embarrassed as I reached-out to stop her fall and caught her in my arms. At first I thought she was angry, but then our eyes met and I realized that she was mostly just startled... and pretty, very pretty!

Once we gained our footing, we introduced ourselves. Her name was Belinda and she hailed from Bloomfield Hills, MI and she was indeed staying at the hotel for the weekend retreat.

Well, at just fifteen years old I was not too experienced with what to do with a pretty young lady at a hotel. But, being the young gentleman I was, I suggested that in order to repay her for my clumsiness, perhaps I could treat her to lunch or something.

She said that was a very nice offer, but she needed to attend a luncheon sponsored by the retreat organizers. However, she said, she and a friend were planning on going to a matinee movie afterward and asked if I would like to join them. "Are you kidding me?" I thought to myself, "This is like winning the Jackpot at Bingo!"

She then asked if I knew of another boy who might want to join us so that her friend would not feel left out. I told her I just might know of such a guy… Fred, have I got a surprise for you!

I don't remember the name of the movie, for all I knew or cared about it could have been the "Sound of Music" released earlier that year. I do recall though that we ate a mountain-full of popcorn and had a lot of fun. About midway through the film, I decided that it was time to make my move.

So, in an incredibly suave and debonair manner, I tactfully raised my right arm as though I was stretching and then gently placed it on the top of her seat back. She seemed to like that, so I dropped it down a bit to her shoulder. With a smile on my face, I kept that arm right there, thinking what a cool dude I had become ever since I turned fifteen years-old just a few days before.

However, after about twenty minutes, all the blood had left my arm. By now it was totally asleep and tingling painfully… I hadn't counted on that. Now, I was really in a quandary.

I knew I had to get that dead arm off of her, but I didn't want her to think I didn't like her or something. And, I had already shown her how clumsy I was back in the elevator, so I sure didn't want to drag it errantly across her body.

So, as the pain increased, a plan came to me. I finally whispered in her ear that I needed to go to the washroom. As she nodded and smiled, I quickly retrieved my weakened appendage using my left arm to assist and headed down the stairs, thanking God for getting me out of that mess.

From then on, I became real careful where I put my arm around girls! On the walk back to the hotel from the theater, I did manage the courage to hold her hand along the way. I didn't get the sense that Fred and his date had hit it off quite as well as Belinda and I had, but I think in the end a good time was had by all on that day in Detroit.

By now you are probably wondering what this innocent little story has to do with my Bat Boy experience on the Detroit road trip. Here goes.

Once we got to Tiger Stadium that night, I began to feel really sick to my stomach and quite dizzy. Maybe it was the rancid butter on all the popcorn I had eaten that afternoon, but whatever it was, I knew I was in bad shape. I told Mr. Berres, the White Sox Pitching Coach who also doubled as our guardian for the trip, about my malady and he gave me cab fare, sending me back to the hotel.

Once I got to the hotel room, I did become violently sick, spending considerable time praying to the porcelain throne in the bathroom. Afterward, I laid out on the bed, still feeling a bit queasy. Thankfully, I quickly fell asleep.

A couple of hours later I woke up, feeling much better, but extremely hungry. It was just before 11:00 p.m. and the hotel coffee shop would soon be closing. So, I threw on some clothes and headed on down. Amazingly, just who would I see sipping on a late night soda in a cozy little booth all by herself? Yes, my sweet Belinda.

Naturally, I joined her and enjoyed a nice meal on my White Sox per diem expense money, recovering fully from the ills of my earlier evening. However, as fate would have it, just as we were getting ready to leave and go our separate ways, who should appear in the lobby but the entire White Sox team returning from their game. Boy, oh boy, did I get the looks and cat-calls that night, now having earned the nickname, Romeo.

Well, now for the lesson. The next day we had a day game scheduled and as soon as I got to the Stadium, Mr. Berres told me that the Manager, Mr. Lopez wanted to see me in his office.

Now, I am sure that Mr. Lopez was normally a very nice man, but you never want to get called into the Manager's office, player or not.

Sox Manager and "My Momentary Mentor" Al Lopez, AKA "El Señor."

As I entered the office, I really didn't know what to think. The incident the night before had been completely innocent and I didn't think much more of it. I really had gotten sick. I really did just happen to run into Belinda at the coffee shop and I really did sleep in my own bed, alone that night. Mr. Lopez seemed to have some differing thoughts on the matter.

The conversation with Mr. Lopez was a one-sided affair. Perhaps, the White Sox six game losing skid was affecting his spirits. Nonetheless, it was clear that he was none too pleased with me and had assumed the worst. He was ashamed of me for having feigned my illness in order to skip out on my job "to go be with that harlot" he said.

I really wanted to set the record straight, but there are times in life when you are just better off keeping your mouth shut, and so I did. I just took the medicine, apologized and left his office wondering just how much trouble I was really in with the team... not exactly the kind of news that dear ol' Mom and Dad would like to hear either.

I took the initiative and called my folks "long-distance" and told them what had happened. I am pretty sure that my Mom believed me. Not sure about my Dad though... I think part of him liked Mr. Lopez's version better. Even as a father, he still had a bit of boy in him too and I think that's what the wink in his eye was saying when I later returned home from the road trip.

A few thoughts occurred to me after that incident. One was that Mr. Lopez probably felt that since the whole team was aware of the situation, he needed to make an example out of me. He couldn't afford to have his players thinking that they could get away with this kind of stuff going forward. In those days, any type of impropriety by a player was dealt with quickly and harshly... usually with a scolding and a fine. Thankfully, Mr. Lopez settled for just the "conversation" with me.

The second thought was about the importance of appearances; some we can control and manage, others we cannot. Quite often in life we are evaluated and judged by what people perceive about us, whether based in fact or not. On that one day, I was just in the *wrong* place at the *wrong* time. For no reason other than that, I would pay some small measurable price to the perception of my character with the team.

The third thought was, "I can't wait to tell my friends what a stud I became in Detroit!"... even Mr. Lopez, the Manager of the Chicago White Sox, had confirmed it! After all, I was a red-blooded American fifteen year-old with surging hormones. Why not improve upon my "reputation" with the home crowd? Well, maybe that wouldn't be such a great idea after all.

Clearly, the grain ran true in Mr. Lopez and I learned from him.

With regards to the actual play on the field, the series in Detroit that weekend went almost as bad as had the two games in New York against the Yankees. After dropping the first two games to the Tigers, it would come down to a Sunday doubleheader to find out if the White Sox could salvage a split of the series.

Back on the mound was our left-hander Tommy John facing the always tough-minded Mickey Lolich for Detroit. Behind the help of an eight run sixth inning which saw Lolich exit the game, John secured the 10-6 win.

This brief moment of elation was short-lived though. Detroit Ace Denny McClain came back in the second contest of the afternoon, posting a complete game win that lasted only 2 hours and 17 minutes, walloping the White Sox 13-2.

The White Sox were now in fifth place, falling seven games behind the American League leading Minnesota Twins.

Fortunately Monday, July 26th was a travel day for the team. Now on to Cleveland!

Municipal Stadium in Cleveland was really an oddity. First, it was one of the early multi-purpose facilities used for both baseball and football having been built in 1931… not an ideal venue for either sport.

Second, it was huge, really huge! For baseball, the stadium had a seating capacity of nearly 74,000 fans, though rarely did their 11,541 average attendance in 1965 ever come close to that capacity level.

In comparison the White Sox were drawing a slightly better average of 13,957 fans per game in 1965. Still, in aggregate both these two venues were impressively pulling in over one million baseball fans per season… a pretty good mark for those days.

Third, this multiplex sports venue in Cleveland for the most part was a really lousy place to watch a baseball game. It was particularly so from the bleachers due to the stadium's sprawling design and location next to Lake Erie (known as the "The Mistake by the Lake") with its biting cold breeze in the spring and fall. And by the way, even for the ball players, the ball park accommodations were pretty abysmal. The Clubhouse was dark, run-down and in general, a pit, especially compared to the facilities at Comiskey.

Although the City of Cleveland issued $3,375,000 in bonds to provide for improvements in 1966 (mainly for the benefit of the Cleveland Browns football team) the facility was still considered outmoded compared to the new stadiums constructed throughout the country.

The centerfield fence was originally constructed so far out that at 470 feet no batter's ball had ever reached the bleachers there on a fly during a game. The solution offered by Bill Veeck in the late 1940s, the then owner of the Tribe, was to erect a temporary fence across the length of the outfield, reigning in the centerfield distance to 410 feet.

Believe it or not, this fence could be moved in or out depending on the game conditions and the opponent. As I recall, the fence wasn't too high, maybe just five or six feet or so. However, that fence was to play a huge part in the formulation of my second best memory on this Cleveland road trip stop... but, more on that later.

The Movable Outfield Wall in Cleveland.
You Can See the Fans Standing Along the Back Side!

Following our travel day from Detroit, we had a scheduled night game, so that provided me the day to explore the city. However, downtown Cleveland was not exactly a paradise back then, so strolling too far from the hotel, even in the daytime was not highly advised. Given my earlier experience that summer near the Robert Taylor Homes in Chicago, I had no interest in a repeat performance!

Equally disturbing was the Cuyahoga River, once described by Time Magazine as "a river that oozes rather than flows." And as a river that occasionally caught fire, that didn't help improve the reputation of the town much either! Thus, visiting the city for the first time, I began to understand the familiar expression spoken in jest about this city that "I spent a week in Cleveland one night!" Thankfully, much of that has changed for the better over the years.

About that time in my young life, I was learning to play the guitar and had mastered a few songs. I learned that there was a big department store close by and that they had a music department. I headed over there as it opened that morning, found a nice instrument to strum on and played to my heart's content.

About twenty minutes into it, who should go walking by but none other than my now dear friends from the Mr. Lefty event , third baseman Pete Ward and centerfielder, Ken Berry! Seems they were on a shopping trip and were just passing by until they caught site of me strumming-up a storm.

They saw me and came into the shop and started to really rock it out with me… what a great moment. They were two of the real gems that I met during *My Year* with the Sox, let me tell you. From that day on, I was no longer known as the "Detroit Romeo" to those Rockers. I was now and forever known to them as "Elvis!"

Ken Berry was a truly great centerfielder. He ran like the wind, had an exceptionally strong arm and did not fear any outfield wall anywhere. Sometimes, he ran a little too hard and would come face to face with one of those fences creating dents on both surfaces, but that was just his style.

In *My Year*, he led the League in fielding percentage for all outfielders. In 1967, he was named to the American League All-Star team. Over his career he also earned two Gold Gloves, but more than any of that, he was a great man who would later as a grandfather write the children's books, *Artie the Awesome Apple* and *Clyde the Clumsy* Oh yes, and just like Pete Ward, the grain sure ran true in that man too!

Ken Berry Feared No Outfield Fence!

Back now to the story about the fence, and my second best memory of the Cleveland road trip.

On this particular night, in fact all three games in Cleveland were scheduled night games, I was shagging baseballs out in left-center, about twenty feet from that temporary fence. Ken walked over and we chatted about our day at the store.

About then, we both noticed a high fly ball coming our way and deep. We both started back, and then began running as we tracked the ball going further and further. I then yelled "I got it!" he said calmly, "I'll take It." I said, "I can get it" and he just said "Take it!" and I *Did*!

As I reached the fence, I jumped as high as I could, put my right hand on top of it and at the peak of my leap, turned back and the ball stuck in my glove! From my momentum, I then began to fall over the fence, but Ken was there to pull me back onto the playing field, hoots and hollers coming from him all the while. He had found a crazy colleague of sorts in me, I guess.

Once on the ground, he gave me a big hug and we ran side by side back to the dugout, with my memory of that wonderful day now forever sealed in my brain. Even more remarkably, "The Catch" as we later would call it, happened just before game-time that night. And yup, the large, gathering crowd saw it all. They too showed their appreciation for the effort and cheered and applauded us all the way back into the dugout. I often wondered what they thought as the BB on my back came into view on my jog off the field! In any case, that was one of the best baseball moments in my life.

However, the results on the field continued to worsen for the White Sox as the slide deepened. In the opening game against the Indians, the White Sox fell 7-3 against the pitching forces of Ralph Terry, who posted a near complete game performance.

In the second game of the three game series, the White Sox were tied with the Indians until the eighth inning. However, they would then surrender two runs in the bottom half of the frame, losing 4-2.

In the final game of the series, the White Sox did salvage a win. Under an extended relief performance by Hoyt Wilhelm and a five RBI offensive breakout performance by catcher, Johnny Romano, the Sox clinched the finale 9-4.

Losing two of three games against the Indians, the White Sox closed out their disastrous road trip with a 2W-7L record, then currently standing in fifth place, eight and one-half games out of first. The White Sox however had a fourteen game home stand awaiting them once they returned to Comiskey Park the next day. Things would improve for them in the coming weeks. In the end, it was one hell of a road trip!

*   *   *

For those of you who might wonder, Belinda and I did meet again a few years later when she was on another retreat; this time in Chicago at the Hilton Hotel. It was great to see her and relive that day from many years before. And no, we never did consummate what Mr. Lopez had assumed we had. Nope, Belinda was not that kind of girl and I was happy for it. You see, the grain ran straight and true in her as well. Just glad to set the record straight, Coach… may you rest in peace, El "Señor."

"El Señor" Al Lopez. (1908-2005)

Hall of Famer Al Lopez was a solid Major League catcher whose record of 1,918 games caught stood for more than forty years until the invention of the revolutionary new double-break hinged catcher mitt developed in the mid-to-late 1960s which made the art of catching a bit more civilized. (NBHOF Library)

Of all dates, Al Lopez was born on 08/08/08 and he lived long enough to endure the Chicago White Sox 88 year World Series Championship drought and see his Boys of Summer take it all in 2005. Unfortunately, the scandalous 1919 White Sox could have won it all too, had they all only tried.

BOTTOM OF THE NINTH

In 1965, the American League was pretty well owned by the Minnesota Twins. The once dominant Yankees had fallen on hard times as I have mentioned. Meanwhile, the White Sox and the Orioles both held out hope of catching the Twins nearly to the end. But by mid-September, all that really remained was a battle for second place. Boy, it sure would have been cool to have been in the World Series, but it was not to be for our crew.

The Twins officially clinched the Pennant on a Jim Kaat win against his former team, the Washington Senators in 2-1 victory. His twenty-five year career all began when he was recruited into professional baseball while attending Hope College located in Holland, Michigan... the same school that my daughter would later graduate from!

Jim Kaat Won 18 Games in 1965, But an Amazing 25 in 1966! You Can Still Hear Jim on MLB TV Where He Continues His Illustrious Long Broadcasting Career. The Grain Runs True in Jim Kaat.

Given the depth of offense and the great pitching they possessed, most folks were shocked that the Twins would lose the World Series to the Dodgers. And, it would be another twenty years before Minnesota recaptured that flag.

For a more detailed recap of the 1965 baseball season, please see the article "A Baseball Fan's Retrospective on the 1965 White Sox Season" located in the Appendix Section. My buddy Mike compiled this and I was happy to contribute to it as well.

As the Sox and Orioles fought for second place, the season began to draw to an end at Comiskey. By the last day of the regular season, the Sox, like me, had come in *Second Place*. Based on pre-season predictions, this was considered a great success overall. Yes, sometimes *Second Place* has its own rewards.

Now the days grew quieter at the Park as fans would find other things to fill their nights and weekends. For us, it was a bit eerie knowing that our time on that great field would soon be coming to an end.

In the last days of *My Year*, I would walk the corridors of the Park and chat with the many vendors and other cast members I had gotten to know over those prior months. All of us shared that uneasy sense that soon the gates to this great enclave of sport would be closed for another season; a trace of fall in the air, with no hope of late October baseball coming our way.

Yet, many of those vendors, security folks, ushers and the rest, would return to this beautiful Park in the spring of 1966 to resume serving both the veteran season ticket holders and a whole new crop of fans. That would not be the case for the six of us shoe-shining Lumber Men.

No, 1966 would bring with it a new Bat Boy Contest and new winners would be named. But to this day, I still try to make a point of being at the last game of the season, wherever I am. There is just something special about it… a sense of camaraderie that transcends the years and the location.

So it was fitting then that on Sunday, October 3, 1965, the

Sox Ace, Joe Horlen would defeat the Kansas City Athletics 3-2 in 2 hours and 9 minutes, before a crowd of just 4,611 fans at Comiskey Park. The great Hoyt Wilhelm earned his twenty-first Save.

The final pitch of the White Sox's season came from reliever Wilhelm's right hand in the top of the ninth inning. That knuckler resulted in a fly ball hit off the bat of Ken "The Hawk" Harrelson and was caught by right fielder Tommie Agee. His following season with the White Sox, Agee would be selected to the American League All-Star team, be named American League Rookie of the Year, and win Gold Glove honors.

But on that Sunday in October, 1965, *My Year* had come to an end.

*   *   *

Then and Now… what a journey I have had with this great Game of baseball.

People often ask me how the ball players of today compare to the ball players back then. Well, that is a hard question to answer since several of the dynamics of the Game have changed somewhat. However, my on-field experience as an active observer of the Game may have provided me with a bit of a unique perspective, so here it goes.

As most fans realize, there are now thirty teams in baseball. That is opposed to the original early modern-day eight team, two league format that comprised the Major Leagues up until the early 1960s when the Leagues expanded to ten teams each.

Now, considerably more aspiring young players have the chance to make it into the professional ranks given the sheer increase in the number of Major League teams. Further, the correspondingly exponential rise in the ancillary supporting professional minor league teams has also allowed more players to go further in the Game.

At the same time, the world has continued to shrink, in a

manner of speaking, so ball players now come from across the globe with the hope of making it in the Bigs. Plain and simple, there is a much larger pool of talented potential ball players now than ever existed back in *My Year*. Still, there are other factors to consider.

The equipment. The baseball gloves and other such equipment do appear to be far superior now, but that old-styled baseball gear did not seem to hamper those guys too much… they just knew how to use what they had and they used it well… just like today.

However, one definite exception was the improvement made to the catcher's mitt. This was actually a revolutionary upgrade that came about in the 1960s with the invention of the double-break hinged design.

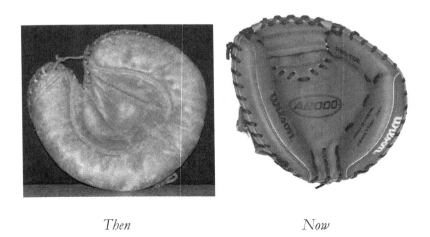

Then   *Now*

Four-time All-Star and three-time Gold Glove catcher Earl Battery has attested that catcher mitts were significantly improving just as he was retiring from baseball in 1967 from the Minnesota Twins. He said, "Today's mitts have multiple breaks and a long oval pocket, more like a first baseman's. When I played, we had a pocket but no breaks, and we caught two-handed so the ball wouldn't pop out." Boy, the grain of toughness sure ran that man!

One-handed catching became possible with the double-break hinged mitt, popularized by Johnny Bench and Randy Hundley in the late 1960s. With this improvement in the catching equipment, a spring-action hinge snapped the mitt closed on contact with the baseball. It also saved a catcher's knuckles from being torn apart and beat-up, by allowing him to place his non-catching hand protectively behind his lower back, thus extending the careers of many a catcher.

The Ball. The ball itself has changed in some characteristics several times over the years too. While its regulated size and weight have stayed the same in the broadest sense, the height of the stitching and the hardness of the ball have fluctuated overtime. The harder the ball and the smaller the stitching, the farther it will travel through the air.

Now back to my earlier story. Way back in baseball time, most pitchers would legally darken the ball with tobacco juice and dirt, and a single ball could last an entire game. However, in 1920, the "dirty ball era" would abruptly come to a tragic end when Cleveland's Ray Chapman was accidentally hit in the head by a pitch from Yankee hurler Carl Mays and subsequently died the next day (no batting helmets in those days!) Reports said that it appeared that Ray had never seen the ball coming his way on that early evening and that it him squarely in his head without any attempt on his part to get out of the way. Truly, one of the most dreadful moments in all of sports.

After that, a rule change was made requiring the umpire to replace a baseball whenever it became "dirty." Baseball folks chewed on that definition for many years before a rule change banned *any* foreign substances from being placed on a game ball. None the less, the "spitball" would continue to be thrown for decades-more as pitchers increasingly found clever ways to "doctor" the ball to give them a further edge against their opponents.

Today, in the modern-day game, once a pitched ball hits the

dirt it is simply and quickly replaced by the umpire. The average life of a baseball in a game today is about six pitches, therefore if an average baseball game goes 250-300 pitches, about forty to fifty balls will be used in typical game.

The Bats. I have fairly well covered the evolution of the bats used in baseball in the opening chapter, so I will not belabor that here. I will say however, that I sincerely doubt that the founders of the Game would be happy to know that sticks of aluminum would one day replace wooden bats in youth, high school and even college baseball. No, for the purest among us, that pinging sound will never replace the true grain of lumber.

Strengthening. Few guys back then strengthened themselves with weight training, whey protein powder or the like. One exception was Tony Conigliaro who even carried dumbbells with him on the road. Despite their apparent lack of emphasis on physical strength training, they were strong, but just naturally so.

When Mickey Mantle was growing up, his father had him work at his lead and zinc mining facility in Commerce, Oklahoma during the summer, just breaking up mindless rocks with a pick and sledgehammer. His father knew exactly what he was doing, as he ingrained a blue-collar work ethic and mentality within his son, while also building out his physical strength beyond imagination. As I mentioned previously, I will never forget the size and strength of Mantle's forearms. In his day, he ran like the wind, and he continued to live up to his first nickname of "The Commerce Comet" given to him by his hometown admirers. Even years later on Major League fields Mantle would easily out-ran his teammates in any competition. As they said, "there were fast runners and then there was "The Mick." Today few players could keep up with him. Overall, he was one exceptionally fast and strong fella… and always a gentleman to me.

Speaking of strong and a gentleman, Ray Fosse, was quite a specimen as a young player. A talented catcher and always a power-hitting threat, he was the first player ever drafted by the

Cleveland Indians in Major League Baseball's first-ever Free Agent Amateur League Draft in 1965. Ray is now a TV announcer for the Oakland A's. I see him at our local meat market sometimes and he is still a horse at sixty-seven years of age... more on Ray later in the book.

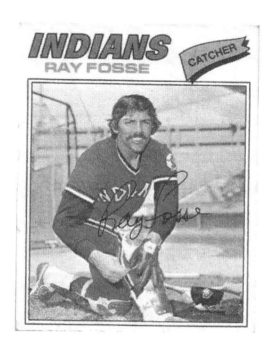

Ray Fosse

Opportunities. Young players now have much more opportunity to play at a high-level at an earlier age. The multitude of youth recreational leagues and travel teams that now crisscross the country with kids younger than age ten is amazing. The resources to help athletes in all sports have flourished enormously.

Professional instruction for kids barely existed back in my era. Now most every kid serious about the Game has a hitting coach, a pitching coach, a catching coach or a fielding coach, along with a personal fitness trainer. Back then, we had dads who had learned from their dads. That was about it until you got into high school or college. Yes, we did have organized baseball for couple of months each summer as I have written about; but the real fun was just between a group of kids that loved the Game.

In our day, we spent our summer days corralling a bunch of neighborhood kids with their gloves, a couple of bats and some balls. We played on a ball fields fabricated in the middle of the street in front of our houses or at a school yard nearby.

Wiffle Ball Home Run Derbies filled our back yards on many nights. No umpires, no coaches, no parents. Just kids having some fun. Nonetheless, we somehow figured-out how to play the Game. Some kids got really good at it too. Just like the kids on the 1964 Pony All-Star team I mentioned earlier.

But, we also didn't have all the distractions kids have today. And, maybe there is just a bit too much, too early for kids today. Many experts suggest that the increase in young Major Leaguers getting hurt may be related to overuse during those formative years.

The Facilities and the Fields. From a facilities and field standpoint, the distance between the bases has remained exactly ninety feet, and the distance between the pitching rubber and home plate is still sixty feet, six inches. However, one notable difference, has been the height of the pitching mound.

In *My Year*, the mound was legally allowed to reach fifteen inches in height, although many teams would fudge on that resulting in reports of mounds up to nineteen inches. However, after Bob Gibson's phenomenal 1968 1.12 ERA season, the mound was officially lowered to ten inches in height in 1969.

Most hurlers did not take kindly to that change. First, because that old height gave them an even greater advantage over the batters. Second, they claimed that it put undue strain on their arms, thereby shortening their longevity. Given the amount of Tommy John surgeries conducted today, they may have had a point. Thus conversations continue even after all this time about raising the mound height yet again to some "reasonable" height.

One set of field dimensions that has been fairly elastic over time has been the distance and the height of outfield fences. Shifting the distance and or modifying the design of the outfield undoubtedly changes the number of home runs and other extra-base hits the field will yield per season. Some parks are known as pitcher's parks, and others as hitter's parks. In *My Year*, most of the ball parks were big.

Top Three All-Time Longest Distance Baseball Outfields (feet)

Longest Center Field	Longest Left Field	Longest Right Field
Polo Grounds (482)	Griffith Park (405)	Crosley Field (370)
Shibe Park (447)	League Park (375)	Wrigley Field (353)
Tiger Stadium (440)	Municipal - K.C. (369)	Comiskey Park (352)

Minimum outfield fence requirements were enacted in 1958 for all ballparks, although the older parks were grandfathered-in, practically every newly constructed ball field can obtain a waiver if they make the request. The stated MLB ballpark dimension regulations seem to be more like guidelines rather than hard and fast rules. Here is the rule:

MLB Rule 1.04, The Playing Field (abridged)
Any Playing Field constructed by a professional club after June 1, 1958, shall provide a minimum distance of 325 feet from home base to the nearest fence, stand or other obstruction on the right and left field foul lines, and a minimum distance of 400 feet to the center field fence.

The height of outfield fences plays a big part in the current formula. Thus, if a team wants a shorter distance from home to the fence, one way to do that is to increase the height of that fence in some proportion to the shorter distance... go figure!

In any case, a rather interesting fact about home runs and outfield fences was that in the earlier part of last century if a baseball skipped over the fence on one bounce it was not a ground-rule double as it is today, but rather a "ground-rule" home run. The rule was later changed during the 1930 National League off-season (American League 1928). The last such "ground-rule" home run was hit by an All-Star catcher playing for the Brooklyn Robins at Ebbets Field on September 12, 1930.

This individual would later go on to manage the Chicago White Sox while I was the Visiting Team Bat Boy at Comiskey Park in 1965. And yes, his name was Al Lopez, "El Señor." At least I sure picked a notable guy to reprimand the Detroit Romeo!

So while there have been many changes to the Game over the years, there are two things that still make this game different than all others, and they are: there is no time limit in this Game and the *defense* controls the ball… pretty sure those things will never change. The consistency of the stats over the years illuminates that the design of this Game was the greatest in the history of sports. Way to go, Abner, et al!

In the final analysis, my take is that the best players would have been good in most any point in time. There are more good players in our current era mostly because there are just more players now and the economics from television revenue and high ticket prices are there to support it.

Bear in mind that all players only directly compete during "their time" in the Game. In the end, greatness can only be fairly measured against the peers of their time and the legacy that one leaves behind from that period. During *My Year*, I had the wonderful opportunity to meet and to become acquainted with some of the best of the bunch, and I certainly remain thankful for all the experiences that I had during that season. That beyond all else, remained foremost in my thoughts as I saw the Bottom of the Ninth come and go in *My Year* and it lingers until this very day.

To support that notion, one guy from that era remains an icon in Chicago to this day... and he is Ken "The Hawk" Harrelson. How strange then that he was the one to make the last out of *My Year* on that fly ball he hit to Tommy Agee.

Naturally, I had carried Hawk's bat on that day and on his previous trips to Chicago. I must say, as I knelt beside him and looked at his chiseled profile those many times, there was no doubt in my mind where his nickname came from! But more amazingly, I never would have imagined that I would still be connected to his legacy all these many years later.

Hawk has lived his whole life in baseball; first as a player, then as a General Manager and now for many years as a renowned broadcaster. His enthusiasm for the White Sox is matched only by his love of the Game itself. His emotional, down-home and witty approach to calling a game is unequalled. Observing him as I have, I am certain that it took him more than a few days to get over making that last out, ending both Kansas City's and Chicago's 1965 season. That's just how deep the grain of the Game runs in that man.

Ken "The Hawk" Harrelson

"Hawk" is known throughout baseball for his descriptive catch phrases such as "You can put it on the board, Yes!" after a Sox home run, "He Gone!" or "Grab Some Bench!" after a strikeout of an opposing player, and "Stretch!" when a White Sox player hits a ball toward the outfield fence.

My wife's favorite Hawk phrase comes after the White Sox have rallied and scored a couple of runs, Hawk will instruct "Don't Stop Now Boys!" He often states that the "Sacks are Packed with Sox" when the bases are loaded, or whines a "Duck Snort" when a softly hit ball floats over the infielder and falls safely in the short outfield for a base hit. Originally called a "Duck Fart" the term was invented and popularized by Hawk when he made the term more family friendly for his television audience. He's also really creative in assigning nicknames to his favorite players such as with "The Big Hurt" for Frank Thomas.

Joined by buddy Tom Paciorek, AKA "Wimpy" (or Hawk's favorite nickname for him, "Wimperoo") was his amusing side-kick for many years. Steve Stone, former pitching great now calls the Sox games with Hawk on Television. The last few years have been rough ones performance-wise for the White Sox and Hawk is always ready to throw a "Dadgummit" your way when something goes wrong for his boys!

You will never see this man leave a game before his team has secured 27 Outs. For him, the bottom of the Ninth is what it's all about. You see for Hawk, until that last out is made, there always was, and there always will be hope for his guys to capture the day.

No, the Ninth Inning has never really ended for some guys. Whether they be players, coaches, instructors, owners, kids and their moms and dads or fans of any description, for some folks the grain of this Game will never end just because of the passage of time… nope, these folks know that even down-big in the Bottom of the Ninth, the Game is still theirs to win. I guess I just might be like one of those guys.

THE PRESSURE OF THE GAME

As much as talent, physical prowess and practice can make a player good, it is how they learn to handle the pressure of the Game that can make the difference in success or failure. The great Hall of Famer Yogi Berra once said, "Ninety percent of this game is half mental" and "In baseball, you don't know nothing." Even after all these years, how true it often is!

My personal favorite Yogism though was when he and a group were chatting about where they should go to dinner. In reference to a particular restaurant that had been suggested by someone in the group, Yogi responded saying "Nobody goes there anymore because it's too crowded."

Got to love Yogi and his classic sayings. He clearly knew about the pressure of the Game and he learned to embrace it. All players should be so fortunate. In the truth, the grain has always run true in that man!

The One and Only, Yogi Berra.
"If You See a Fork in the Road, Take It!"

To make the point about the impact of pressure in the Game, the following brief scenario may help provide a glimpse of what our heroes face each day they go to work.

So, it is a bright and early Monday morning. You had a busy weekend, struggling to complete a pending deadline on a major project for your Company. The Company has been going through some performance troubles and they are really counting on **you** to right the ship.

You pull into the parking garage and head towards your office. Getting there early, you hope to get a head start on the day. The work you put in over the weekend hadn't produced any significant results, so you *really* want to move quickly in getting the project defined and ready for presentation to your bosses. However, as you round the corner to your cubicle, three co-workers are already standing there waiting to pick your brain on *their* projects.

Being the good guy and leader that you are, you take time to help them first, but now time is getting away from you. Finally, with only minutes to spare, you sit down at your desk ready to perform. But just then, you feel a searing warmth coming from behind. You turn to see a panel of bright lights locked in on you. Behind the lights, cameras are whirling. A crowd gathers and grows. They know **you** need to save the day and want to see **you** pull that rabbit out of your hat like you have done before. They believe in you, and **you** just might be their only hope for survival. They begin to chant your name, then louder and louder. There is a lot at stake and they know it. So do you... **You** *feel* it?!!!

Now the television monitor across the way is showing the action in your cube... you see yourself as beads of perspiration fill your brow. You learn that the broadcast is also being shown simultaneously in the Board Room where the executive management team is tuned in, anxiously awaiting the completion of your project. You survey the office and see that all eyes are on you. One co-worker mentions that your wife, kids and parents changed their plans for the day and are on the way to see *you* save the Company. And now, you are down to just a few moments to pull off the Company-saving effort. You reflect on the mission before you. Heads-down you launch into the work you have been mulling over. You type as fast you can think, but you are falling behind. The tension is becoming intense as the clock ticks away and then, just like that, it is over… your time is up. Did *you* hit the ball out of the park, or did the *Pressure* send you and your team to the showers?

Well, in *My Year* I saw a lot of days like that around the Clubhouse. Just imagine having to perform your job under that level of scrutiny every day, and before a live, raucous crowd of forty thousand fans and millions more watching and listening on television and radio. That might give you a glimpse at the kind of pressure our baseball idols cope with each and every day at their workplace.

One crucial insight that I gained about mid-season in *My Year,* is that this Game, played at this level, is really a grind. A month of daily workouts, being coached and re-coached while playing hard for thirty or so games in the Spring to earn or to keep your roster spot. Months of training and conditioning before even being extended that opportunity. Then 162 grueling games during the regular season. And hopefully, all that work under pressure will lead you to another month of even more intensity in the post-season.

By mid-August your body is racked with pain, your mind rewinds every play, every pitch, every moment until your brain can no longer process it all. You are almost spent, finished. Except for you, your personal love of the Game presses you onward, praying that a mid-season slump will pass you by.

Unlike any other professional sport, baseball is a marathon composed of daily sprints linked along an enormously lengthy and emotionally charged season. The incessant travel… three days here, two nights there, even at home you are living out of a suitcase. Day after day, week after week, month after month, it wears on you.

Maybe two days in thirty to call your own and the balance

spent keeping your job... honing your skills both physically and mentally, until you get to the point where for a while all you can do is react to a day that seems a lot like the one before. But no, today is the only day that matters for now. Today, you *must* perform yet again. The grind continues.

Oh, and yes, the competition comes not only from your opposing team, but also from the guy in Triple A just waiting for you to lose your way. And let's not forget that while not considered a "contact sport" per se, there is plenty of physicality that can zap your strength and mental prowess in this Game. In fact, this Game is not for the faint of heart... a head first slide into home can prove that.

Pressure is a funny thing. I saw great players who would weep after going 0/4 in *one* game. I saw others who would go 0/30 at the plate and the only way you would know it was if you read it in the newspaper. It's all about your make-up... how **you** handle it. The tension, the pressure, the fear of failure... the allure of success. Yes, I repeat, day after day, week after week and month after month it continues... and it builds.

I saw pitchers who were lights-out for four games in a row and then were barely able to retire a batter for their next two games. Some, like All-Star Steve Blass pitched as an ace for eight years with Pittsburgh until in 1972, when he suddenly and inexplicably completely lost his control and couldn't find the strike zone. Within a year, that would end his career.

Steve Blass

Once known as the "Steve Blass Disease" many great competitors, position players and pitchers alike, have developed what later would be called "the Yips" or "the Thing." Pressure, when improperly applied can be a sorrowful thing indeed. Sadly, the Yips can occur at any age or level of player. It not only affected baseball players like Blass and Steve Sax, but also notable golfers such as Slamming Sam Sneed, Bernhard Langer and Ben Hogan and other sportsman as well; even Cricket players!

Fortunately, the condition often disappears on its own over time and there are some treatments available now for severe cases. In fact, I still have moments of it when I go to throw a ball in a public venue like throwing a foul ball back to a player on the field. In spite of all the throwing I did with Phil Ortega, my long-toss buddy from the Washington Senators, I just lock-up at times. **Pressure.**

Now, some guys were warhorses and some were not. The intensity of some, like Jimmy Piersall are well-chronicled for his many on and off the field antics, later portrayed in the movie **Fear Strikes Out**. Suffering through bi-polar disease, Jimmy still somehow was able to play *seventeen* years in the Bigs.

Actor Anthony Perkins (R) Portrays Jimmy Piersall in "Fear Strikes Out."

Another observation I have made about this Game is that success does not always breed success. I saw some players who were having a stellar start to their season and in reward, were named to the All-Star team. Then, for some unknown reason, they played miserably for weeks or even months after the big game. For some, trying to live up to their star status was actually a curse. **Pressure**.

Yup, the same can happen to a whole team. Many teams who are leading their league half way through the season will sometimes fall on hard-times for no apparent reason. Meanwhile, teams that have started the season poorly will sometimes seemingly come out of nowhere and win the World Series. **Pressure.**

Such could be said of the two Major League teams in my neck of the woods in 2014. For whatever reasons, the Oakland A's would collapse that August while the San Francisco Giants would re-group and rise to the occasion for post season play. Winning the 2014 World Series, over the Kansas City Royals, who themselves had risen above their regular season performance, was a classic example of *how* to handle pressure... not so much for my anemic Athletics however. Their collapse in 2014 rivaled some of the greatest breakdowns in baseball history.

Some of the other most monumental team collapses over the years were the 1951 Brooklyn Dodgers, the 1964 Philadelphia Phillies, the 1978 Boston Red Sox, the 1987 Toronto Blue Jays, the 1995 California Angels, the 2007 New York Mets, and the 2009 Detroit Tigers. But as a Chicago native, the one pressure induced team collapse I remember most was the absolute free-fall of the 1969 Chicago Cubs, along with the corresponding meteoric rise of the New York Mets.

The Amazing 1969 NY Mets Won It All!

In the first season after the American and National Leagues were each split into two Divisions, the East and the West, the Chicago Cubs began the 1969 season winning eleven of their first twelve games. The Cubs were now in the newly formed National League East Division and in first place from the start of the season, never slipping into second place through the All-Star break.

Even after the All-Star break, the Cubs continued to build their lead to nine games as late as August 16ᵗʰ, with just forty-two games remaining in the season. However, at the start of September, the Cubs somewhat unexpectedly went into an eight game losing streak. When the team finally emerged with a win on September 12th, they found themselves 2-1/2 games behind the fledgling New York Mets. Amazingly, the Cubs would never regain first place that season.

The Cubs had stingily held onto first place in the National East Division for 155 consecutive days and 143 games during the 1969 season. Nevertheless, they then went on to lose seventeen of their last twenty-five games!

Meanwhile, the New York Mets had surpassed them in the critical home stretch by winning twenty-three out of their last thirty games of the season. Leo "The Lip" Durocher's Cubs would finish 92-70, while Gil Hodges' Miracle Mets won 100 games that season, winning the National League East by eight games.

The New York Mets would subsequently sweep the Atlanta Braves in the National League Championship Series, and then go on to win the World Series against the Baltimore Orioles in five games.

I think a lot of it is how each player handles pressure and how as teammates, they interact with each other. As I mentioned, Little Louie sure could keep a Clubhouse loose, but it's even more than that.

If a team is made up of talented players and coaches that support and nurture each other throughout their individually tough times, they will often be able to gel as even more talented, but less self-supporting clubs might crumble.

In support of that notion, the Mets 1969 Manager, Gil Hodges, was largely credited with their turnaround, having skillfully platooned his players by using every man in his dugout in order to keep them all fresh and ready for the final stretch run. Rightfully so, Hodges was named *The Sporting News'* Manager of the Year.

The Beloved "Miracle Worker" Gil Hodges.

However, in the case of the 1969 Cubs, most folks feel that their collapse came as a direct result of the overriding and ever-pressure-filled antics placed upon them by none other than their own Manager, Durocher.

Attributed as having coined the phrase "Nice guys finish last" Leo was a hard-driving near-tyrant whose aggressive style might have fit better on a football field than in a baseball Clubhouse. Yes, he did have his successes in baseball having won three pennants, and one World Series over his twenty-four year managerial career. However, his temperament only became more abrasive as he aged in the Game. As if to prove the point, he was once quoted saying:

"If I were playing third base and my mother were rounding third with the run that was going to beat us, I'd trip her. Oh, I'd pick her up and brush her off and say, 'Sorry, Mom,' but nobody beats me."

Leo Durocher was eventually fired by the Cubs, mid-season in 1972.

It is true that the spotlight can be a wonderful thing and the rewards for success can be enormous in this Game. But, like the struggling actor who works as a barista while honing his craft, there really are very few baseball players who are overnight successes.

Years of struggling in the minor leagues is not a great way to spend your time in waiting, but for most, that is their only way to the Bigs. The competition is fierce, the lifestyle is especially grueling and no one really cares if you make it to the next level but you and perhaps your mom and dad.

But like Tom Hanks' movie character Manager Jimmy Dugan states to his players in the 1992 fictionalized film account of the real-life All-American Girls Professional League during World War Two years, "It's *supposed* to be hard. If it wasn't hard, everyone would do it. The hard… is what makes it great."

So, if you are going to make *your* way to the Show, you REALLY need to be an *exceptional player* and you must REALLY want it… almost to the exclusion of everything else in your life. And, you REALLY need to know how to handle PRESSURE in productive ways. Maybe then, just maybe you might get your shot.

Geena Davis (no relation) and Tom Hanks in "A League of Their Own."

During *My Year*, the guys that I saw who were best at handling pressure in productive ways were the guys who just laughed at themselves when things got tough. Sure, they took their failures seriously and weren't happy when they went 0 for whatever or pitched a miserable game. But those guys somehow always remembered that baseball *is* a game of failure. The best of the bunch fail seven out of ten times when they go to the Plate. However, if properly applied, *failure* can be your friend. More on that later in the book.

Expecting perfection in this Game is just a formula for begetting more failure. And yet, many did, throwing temper-tantrums that would lead to downward spirals. In this Game, a short memory is a good thing. Just forget about the nasty yesterday you had and go have a ball today... that's the ticket!

From what I saw of the players, inner confidence, a pure belief in yourself and not taking the Game too seriously seemed to be important traits in beating down the pressure. Guys like Phil Ortega, just loved every day they got the chance to put on a Big League uniform. They kept the Game just that, a *game*... and they probably would have played it for little more than meal money.

*   *   *

These days, I spend a lot of time watching high school and college kids playing baseball. I love the purity of it. I love that these kids have dreams and they work really hard striving to get to the next place in their journey. They can't even imagine what it's truly like in the Bigs, but they give it their all to try and find out.

Most will fall by the wayside. Some will get their shot. Most will never set foot on a Major League field. Yes, as great as this Game is, it can be a cruel one at times too. In truth, the difference between moving up or moving out is pretty minute, and luck and timing beyond one's own control do play a big part in it. More on that a little later.

Still, it is a joy to see a good kid make his way to the Show, and I have seen a few complete that journey. One on his way is Kris Bryant, so just keep an eye on that kid. Unless the system screws him up or he gets hurt, he is the real deal!

Kris, the 2013 College Player of the Year, was the second overall pick in the 2013 Major League Armature Draft out of the University of San Diego. (Stanford pitching ace, Mark Appel took the number one Draft spot.) That year as a Junior, Kris lead the NCAA with 31 homers in just 58 games; and that with the recently introduced and deadened, BBCOR bat.

Continuing his pace-setting trends, Bryant was named the 2014 Minor League Player of the Year. And, with a .364 batting average and a league-leading six homers, he was also named the MVP of the 2013 Arizona Fall League.

*2014 Top Prospect, Kris Bryant Hit 43 Homers
With a .325 Average in AAA.*

So that kid can play. But, more importantly, by all accounts he is a really decent person as well. Recently, he donated a signed gamer to a fan known only as Mike who otherwise was going to pay a scalper a tidy sum for a similar one. When Mike wrote Kris just to verify the authenticity of that bat, Kris was a bit upset by the situation and just sent the unsuspecting Mike a real treat... one of his gamers!

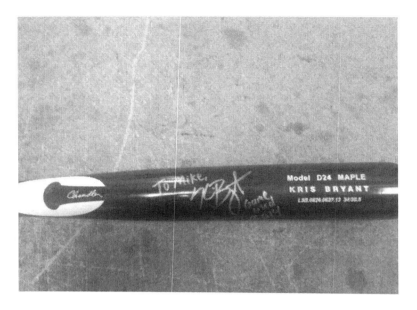

Game-Used Bat Gifted to a Random Guy Named Mike;
Just One of Bryant's Many Fans.

As I said, if this young man stays healthy and the Cubs bring him along correctly, a new superstar may rise. In any case, clearly the grain runs true in Kris Bryant.

So, when parents ask me if they should encourage their kid to become a Big Leaguer, I tell them what I did. I tell them that I supported my son in doing whatever he was passionate about in life. However, I never encouraged him to take the game he loved to play beyond the day when it was no longer fun to walk on the field. After all, for 99.7% of the kids that play the Game, that is what it should be... fun.

That doesn't mean that every day is supposed to be a blast. Hard work, like Jimmy Dugan said, is part of what it takes to excel at this Game. My son sure did that.

No, it's more that when the joy to participate at the level you are at comes at a bigger cost than the benefits received *over some reasonable time period*, then that's when the fun part is waning.

Whether it be due to injury, reaching your peak as a player or all the sacrifices needed to participate that just outweigh what you get from those moments on the field, then that is the time to consider moving on. That's what I told my kid... that's what he did.

That day comes to every player at some point and on that day, it is probably best to just hang-up those competitive spikes and begin learning how to enjoy the Game from off the field... or, become a coach or a broadcaster!

*Even the Greats Like Derick Jeter and Paul Konerko
See the Day When They Hang-up Their Spikes.*

*   *   *

So, beyond what I have stated thus far, just what is it that makes this Game so hard? Well, from what I saw nothing can truly prepare you for playing this Game at the Major League level. No amount of youth travel ball, high school ball, college ball or even minor league play can adequately prepare you for the *grind* of being a Big League player.

Simply stated, baseball at the Major League level is first and foremost a **business,** and a pretty tough one at that. Up until you reach that level, it has all been a surreal journey of hard work, fun, hope, lots of camaraderie and some "friendly" competition played at a progressively higher echelon as your skills improved. But once money becomes involved, the mission takes a swift and drastic turn.

Now you really *are* just a number with a name attached, a piece on a chessboard easily sacrificed for reasons you may never know. It goes beyond your stats. Playing well? *Everybody* at that level plays well. What's your edge? How will you earn your keep? How will the bean counters factor you in? How do the fans "like" you?... it might matter less than you think with *these* chess masters making the moves. Just watch the 2011 movie ***Moneyball*** and you will gain great insight into what the *real* professional Game is all about. A thin skin will not provide you with any comfort on those ball fields, of that I am certain.

Being able to adjust to that reality and still keep one's childlike love of the Game is a big hurdle. In *My Year*, this awakening was perhaps the most bitter of all pills for me, an idealistic and dreamy-eyed kid to accept about the Game... in the Bigs, it is a business, not a fairyland, although dreams still can come true for those who are lucky enough, tough enough and determined enough to meet the challenge. Just reflect on all the great players I have discussed herein as proof. Somehow, they all learned to first embrace, and then to carry-out that transition. Here is just one more example... 2014 Baseball Hall of Fame Inductee and my son's favorite player while growing-up, Frank Thomas.

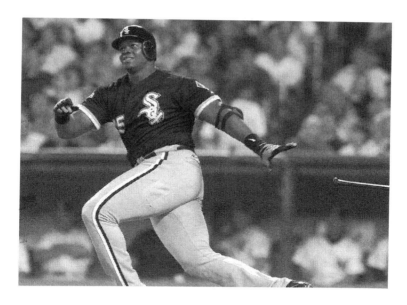

The "Big Hurt" Frank Thomas Fought Hard to Reach
the Top of the Mountain

Looking at Frank's massive size, strength and overall athleticism, one might be tempted to think that the Big Hurt would have had a cakewalk on his way to the Show... but that was far from the case.

Even a great star like Frank found the road to the Major Leagues an immense challenge. As he documented in the Forward he wrote for the 1999 book, **Great Practices, Great Games: Coaching Youth Baseball** by Dr. John Mayer and renowned Hitting Instructor and Coach Steve Hayward, Frank encountered many challenges on his pathway to stardom. Frank wrote: "Most fans see me at the plate, attacking pitches and doing my job as a professional ballplayer. What they haven't seen are the many obstacles that I have faced just to get the opportunity to stand up at the plate... In sports, I have always loved baseball first: but, like many of the loves in one's life, great disappointment has accompanied great success."

Frank goes on to document that even with his intense passion for the Game, he was not drafted by a single major league team out of high school, nor was he offered a baseball scholarship to any university. Despite great performances while in college (he attended Auburn University on a football scholarship but also played baseball there) and in the 1987 Pan Am Games, he wasn't invited to be on the US Olympic team. Throughout all stages of the Minor's he fought for his place and even though he had great statistics while there and at Spring Training in 1990, he still wasn't brought up to the White Sox Big League squad to start that season. He commented: "My whole career seemed like a case of working to climb the mountain harder than anybody else, and yet never becoming king of the hill." His response was to work only harder and to not give up.

Blessed with parents and coaches that stood by him, Frank finally got his chance when on August 2, 1990, he donned his first White Sox Major League uniform. A few weeks later, he launched the first of what would become just one of 521 career home runs. Over his nineteen year career he was a two-time AL MVP, a five-time All-star selectee and finished his career with .301 batting average among his many accomplishments.

But above all else, is the man. On his induction day into the Hall, Frank, in his emotionally-packed speech, took the time to thank each and every notable person that helped him reach the top of that mountain, one by one, each by name!

As he concluded his speech Frank said "To all you kids out there, just remember one thing from today, there are no shortcuts to success. Hard work, dedication, commitment… stay true to who you are." Yes, the grain runs true *and* deep in Frank Thomas.

From what I saw in *My Year* and throughout all my experiences with baseball, it is just time spent living with that level of intensity that will test the measure of a man for this Major League version of the Game. Whether one can actually handle the tremendous strain and still excel, day after day, week after week, month after month and year after year… now that is a real challenge. Do that, and you have learned how to handle Big League **Pressure.**

To have the talent, temperament, grit and luck to become a Major Leaguer… hmmm, amazing. But just imagine what it takes to rise to *stardom* in *that* Company. **Incredible!**

So yes, "The Hard **Is** What Makes it Great."

EXTRA INNINGS

The year 1965 was a most memorable one for me, as I am sure you can imagine. I gained so much that year, had such fun and clearly had experiences that have lasted a lifetime. I also grew up quite a bit that summer, having survived some tough realities of life. So many people gave so much to me that year and I will forever be indebted to the Chicago White Sox family.

However, after *My Year* in the Game and all the experiences I had, I needed some time to sort it all out and just get back to being a regular kid for a while. Like most of my teenage friends, my interest in baseball was largely replaced by an interest in cars and girls for the balance of my time in high school and college.

Sure, I would still watch games on television once in a while. But in a way, being so intimately involved with the behind the scenes aspect of the Game at such an early age kind of tarnished me in a way... much like when Dorothy first saw the Wizard hiding behind that magic curtain in Oz, I would suppose.

In fact, I did not attend another Major League baseball game in person until the 1984 All-Star game in San Francisco, and that was as the guest of the Fairmont Hotel... boy, you should have seen that tailgate party! White linen tablecloths with steak and lobster served by waiters in tuxedos and black tie, all presented elegantly on a carpeted section of the parking lot at ol' Candlestick Park. At times, my job back then did have its perks!

One day a few years later, my then four year old son Chris picked-up a baseball and tossed it to me. When I tossed it back to him, a big smile covered his little face as he said "Again Daddy!" My long hiatus from our national pastime was about to end. Yes, in that one instant the grain of the Game once again captured me, holding on steadfastly ever since. As I said at the start of our journey, this Game just has a way of doing that.

*   *   *

Yes, I have learned many things over the years as a student of the Game. However, just when you think you have seen it all, something new pops-up and you are reminded just how special this "pastime" really is. Just like Yogi said… "In baseball, you don't know nothing!"

One lesson I came to know through the years is that professional baseball is truly a highly connected community as I have demonstrated many times throughout this book. However, here is another example I would like to share.

In 1979, Bud Selig was one of the owners of the Milwaukee Brewers. That year, he signed Ray Fosse (my butchers acquaintance, remember?) to his last Major League contract. Unfortunately, multiple injuries were to soon end Ray's playing days and he turned to broadcasting for his livelihood, his playing days then over.

In 1998, Bud was named as the Ninth Commissioner of Baseball. Also in 1998, Cal Ripken ended his all-time consecutive game record. As Commissioner, Selig led the public praise for Cal's accomplishments as he retired that year. More on Cal later.

In 2002, the All-Star Game was played in Selig's hometown of Milwaukee. The company I worked for had purchased some premium seats intended to be given to a number of top clients, along with some of our execs. As it turned-out, one of our guys needed to cancel the day before and my boss asked if I would like to attend.

I was a bit torn at first because my son had a high school game of his own that same night. In fact, up until then, I had only missed one of his games since he was six years old, and on that night he hit a home run and pitched a great game as a twelve year old. So I did have a bit of trepidation in missing this one. However, my daughter really thought I should go and she volunteered to video tape her brother's game for me. So off I went.

As it turned out, it was quite fortuitous as this game was to become one of the most famous, or perhaps infamous, of all Major League All-Star Games. And, I was seated no more than thirty feet from the Commissioners' entourage.

The game itself was pretty exciting too, with lots of offense. The game was tied 7-7 after nine innings, and remained tied at that tally after the bottom of the eleventh inning. Since the managers wanted to make sure that each player got a chance to play in the game, neither side now had any players left on their benches. Concerned for the arms of the pitchers currently on the mound, Selig made the controversial decision to declare the game a tie, much to the dissatisfaction of the fans. Selig later said that this call was "embarrassing" and that he was "tremendously saddened" by the outcome of the game.

Well, it was pretty cool to be able to see all that hoopla at such a close range. The outcome of that game changed the All-Star Game forever. What a night!

Commissioner Selig in Milwaukee, 2002.

And the best part? Well, my son hit a homer, a double off the wall and pitched a shutout that night. Thanks to my daughter, I was able to watch that game to my hearts-content!

My Son Chris After
Pitching a Perfect Game.

My Daughter Ashley
Celebrating a Birthday.

I now live in the San Francisco Bay Area and have become a bit of an Oakland Athletics fan. Now, not to worry… thanks to MLB.TV I am still able to listen to and watch my Sox too! As much as I like the Northern California broadcast teams, there is a special humor and grand history that still makes watching or listening to the White Sox game-callers special… these guys are great!

Ed Farmer and Darrin Jackson Call the White Sox Games on Radio.

Hawk and Stoney Call the White Sox Televised Games.

So what does Ray Fosse have to do with all this? Well, Mr. Selig announced in 2014 that this would be his last year as the Commissioner. On August 19, 2014 Ray Fosse, now a long-time television announcer for the Athletics, lead an on-air interview of his former boss Selig, some thirty-five years later, reminiscing on their times in baseball together. Joining Ray with Bud was broadcast partner, Glen Kuiper.

Glen Kuiper and Ray Fosse

Glen and his brother Duane, a former Major League second baseman and now the voice of the San Francisco Giants, grew up on a farm near Racine Wisconsin. Their father bought his cars from a nearby dealership. That dealership was owned by Bud Selig's father! And, even more spooky, as I recall, my college roommates went to Case High School in Racine; that would have put them in Duane's graduating class!

Oh, and one more crazy coincidence to pass along… guess who The Hawk called-out in the recent ALS Ice Bucket Challenge? None other than his former teammate from the Cleveland days and yes my butcher's friend, Ray Fosse!

Yup, some things about this Game are just down-right amazing; and so intimately connected! The love of the Game and the straightness of their Grain has never left each of these players, turned broadcasters.

The Brothers Kuiper

Duane is a seven-time Emmy winner as a broadcaster. He also still holds the Major League record for having the most number of At-Bats while generating just one home run over his career. Not much of a power threat, but Duane was a first-class defensive player and his career batting average was .271. He has also watched his beloved San Francisco Giants win three World Series Titles in the past five years... a fabulous run indeed!

*   *   *

As is sometimes the case in life, sadness can catch you unexpectedly. In the early fall of 1965 we learned that my Mom had breast cancer. Back in those days, the measures to attempt to cure it were few and very radical.

Through the grace of God, my Mom, while suffering greatly for a time, did survive and went on to live a full life until she passed quietly in the night at 82 years of age. She had also survived lung cancer later in life, so I guess you could say that she was one tough ol' broad!

My Dad died way too young from lung cancer at age 67. Really a shame. He would have loved getting to know my beautiful and successful daughter Ashley and watching my highly accomplished son Chris, himself a Youth All-Star and All-Conference Baseball Player in high school, play the Game. My kids are amazing people, so such a loss for all concerned.

The summer after his death, my Dad's golf buddies had a tree planted on his home course in his honor. He was, as I said, a nice man and he is well-remembered.

By the way, tobacco, whether smoked, sniffed or chewed, does kill. That ever-present cigar and it's wafting smoke that filled my childhood home eventually did my Dad in... almost six months to the day after his diagnosis.

The recent loss of the great Hall of Famer, Tony Gwynn to salivary gland cancer confirms that it was actually a blessing that Norm Cash had so blatantly turned me off to chewing tobacco, though I doubt that was his intent. I did however smoke cigarettes for many years before finally overcoming that awful addiction. Yes, the choices we make will eventually hold us accountable.

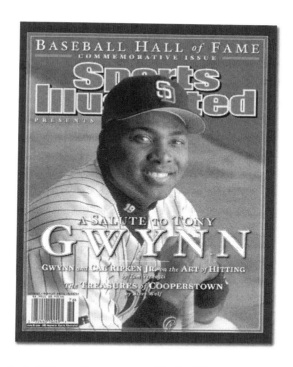

"Mr. Padre" Tony Gwynn was a Hall of Famer in All Regards.

*   *   *

It is also sad to report that 1966 was the last year of the Chicago White Sox Bat Boy Contest. I was later told that more problems arose with the continued deterioration of the neighborhood around Comiskey Park. More threatening incidents similar to what I had experienced on the Dan Ryan Expressway overpass that past summer helped lead the White Sox in their decision to end the Daily News Contest.

Apparently, having young boys from differing parts of the metropolitan area get to the Southside Bastion of Baseball became too much of a potential liability for the Sox to maintain and the Contest Days were gone. However, it was a great run and I have seen many posts from other White Sox Bat Boys who had participated in the Contest over the years. Each one expressed their appreciation to the White Sox for giving kids like us the time of our young lives. Accordingly, going forward older and more street-wise kids got their chance on that grand field. I have often wondered if Sharkey finally got to do the hiring before his retirement in 1967.

I also am proud and fortunate to have been pictured in the last White Sox Bat Boy Chicago Daily Newspaper promotional piece. The one below was signed by Bill "Moose" Skowron nearly forty-five years later and is dearly prized. Here's how that promotional newspaper ad happened to become signed by Moose, all those many years later.

Promo Clipping from the Chicago Daily News in 1966,
the Last White Sox Bat Boy Contest Ever.

In 2008, quite by coincidence, I met a gal named Julie Taylor at a social event. Julie headed the Customer Relations team at US Cellular Park, the replacement stadium for old Comiskey/White Sox Park. She was sporting a World Series Ring from the 2005 White Sox team when I met her... dainty and lady-like did not describe the monstrous gems bestowed by Sox owner, Jerry Reinsdorf... it was HUGE and it dwarfed Julie's small hand.

A 2005 White Sox World Series Ring.

The "11-1" represents the Sox Post-Season Playoff Record of 11 Wins with Only 1 Loss. On the opposite side, the players name and jersey number would be scribed, along with the White Sox 99-63 Season Record.

Once we got to know each other a bit, I mentioned my history with the Sox to her. I showed her some of the pictures and news clippings from back then and she had an idea.

After his playing days, Moose, a Chicago native, became an ambassador for the team. One night, Julie arranged for me to reunite with Moose at the "Cell" as it is now called.

I brought along the press clipping with Moose and Mickey in it and another picture of us from when we were heading out on our Road Trip. My brother Larry and a friend, who was also named Julie, joined me.

I can't say that Moose exactly remembered me or even the context of the pictures. Yet, he was kind enough to sign the pictures from the gone-by era and take a new one with me too.

Moose passed in April, 2012 and he is missed. I am very thankful to Julie for making our reunion possible. That sure made it seem like my time with the White Sox had come full-circle.

Even more sad than the end of the White Sox Bat Boy Contest, was the loss of the Chicago Daily News itself in 1979. The News was an afternoon paper and like many of its counterparts across the nation, it could not maintain profitable circulation levels. Even having the great Mike Royko as its featured columnist could not revitalize the once great Chicago Daily News.

Mike Royko Chicago Daily News—1972 Pulitzer Prize —Commentary.

*   *   *

As I wrote this Memoir, I could not help but reflect upon the memory of my cousin Gary who passed way too young a few years back. Gary was a great guy and an enthusiastic baseball fan. The grain in him may have taken him down some unusual pathways in his short life, but never a truer man was there.

While he was an avid Yankee fan, he and his brother Chris drove all the way from New Jersey to see me on the field at Comiskey one weekend. As I mentioned previously, he and other family members and a few of his friends also came to see, and cheer for me at Yankee Stadium when I was there. Boy, that sure felt good!

Later, Gary told me that seeing me on the field at Yankee Stadium was one of his greatest memories. Well, in turn Gary was responsible for providing my family and me with a grand memory as well, some years later. Here's how.

Each year, Gary and a friend would trek to Baltimore to watch the Yankees play the Orioles at their Park at Camden Yards. We were living in Maryland back then and Gary had gotten some extra tickets, so we joined him for the game... and what a game it turned out to be! Not only did we get to see Mariano Rivera secure his 36th and final save of the season, but the date was September 20, 1998 and baseball history was about to be made.

We had great seats, just beyond third base. During warm-ups, we noted that Cal Ripken was not taking infield practice, but that was not really all that unusual. What was unusual was that when the game began, he still hadn't come out to his position at third.

For a moment, the crowd went silent. Then a buzz began circling Camden Yards as one fan after another realized that this was the night that Cal had decided to end his all-time consecutive game playing streak at 2,632 games; a record that will never be surpassed.

Much like the night of September 6, 1995 when he set the new record for consecutive games played surpassing the immortal Lou Gehrig's previous mark of 2,130 consecutive games, the crowd stood and erupted in unison cheering Cal, Cal, Cal! And as on that prior night, Cal paid the fans his respects with a ceremonial walk around Orioles Park, high-fiving his adoring admirers all along the way.

I must say, that was one of the most thrilling moments that I had experienced at a ballpark in my entire life. The fact that my kids were there to see it too made it only that much more special. Oh without doubt, the grain runs true and deep in that gentleman from Maryland.

The Iron Man Cal Ripken, Jr.

His 2,632 Consecutive Game Playing Streak ended Sunday, September 20, 1998 and my family and I were there to see it, thanks to my Cousin Gary. The Grain sure runs deep in the Ripken clan.

Recalling back to that night at the 2002 All-Star game in Milwaukee for a moment, it happened that Cal was there too! No, not as a player, but now as a celebrity, as he had retired in 2001.

As I was returning from the concession stand before the game, I had the chance to walk side-by-side with the Iron Man along the concourse for a few minutes. I even shared my popcorn with him as other fans sought his autograph. I told him that I was at Camden Yards on the night he sat down and how great that was to see. He just smiled and said "Thanks for being there" as he was then lead away by the crowd.

Thanks Gary, for all of that and for always calling me "Cuz."

*   *   *

My Year, 1965. It was a time when personal integrity, responsibility and accountability still counted. When "doing the right thing" and "Truth, Justice and the American Way" still stood tall.

Yet, those principles would soon be tested. It is no secret that the late 1960s ushered in a new era that would challenge those hallowed principles to their very core.

The country and the Game were to suffer mightily in the coming decades as a way of life struggled to re-define itself. Even the Game itself was in jeopardy of losing its way through the turmoil and strife of the 1970s, 1980s and 1990s. Player strikes and owner lockouts threatened to destroy this great Game forever. But in the end, the Grain of this Game ran deep, very deep. And True. The principles that I observed in *My Year* did in fact endure and have indeed moved the Game back to its very soul.

As for me, I have lead a very full life. I was blessed to have a decent career, mostly as a sales and marketing executive in the computer software business. The values I learned growing-up in my era stuck with me, and I worked to put them to good use the best I could along the way, both in my career and in my personal life.

Sure, I have had plenty of failures along the way too. But as *My Year* taught me, failure is just one of the inescapable realities of life, as I have stated. It is how we handle it that makes the difference in our succeeding or not *over time*, just like ball players need to learn how to handle the pressure they face in their profession.

In fact, as I stated before, I learned that failure is a gift. It prepares us for the next great things in our life. Without failure to guide us along the way, at some point our mistakes may become overwhelming. Here's a little story to help demonstrate that point.

I once had a boss many years ago, whose boss was an exceptionally successful businessman. I knew him of course, and while I never worked directly for him, he seemed like a decent guy. I will call him Ben, because strangely enough, that was actually his name!

Ben made tons of money and he earned all that went with it. However, the company he partly owned (and that I worked for at the time) had expanded too quickly by taking some uncalculated risks. At one point they hit a major cash-flow crunch. After refinancing in every way they could, one day their bank called-in their loan. All of the owners met and realized they had no choice but to fold.

I had been through such events before, so while I wasn't happy about having to find new employment, I took it in stride and moved on. About six months later, I ran into Ben at a Sunday Brunch at our local Marriott Hotel. He, like me, was there with his family.

As I stood next to him in the carving line, tears welled-up in his eyes as he profusely apologized to me, of all people, for his failure. He then shocked me again by saying that he was now lost, his identity was gone.

I asked him why, and with his voice cracking he said that this was the first time in his *entire fifty seven years* that he had ever failed. Now I was really shocked. All those years and he never got the benefit of failing? "Obviously," I thought to myself, "he must never have had played the game of baseball during his youth!" In fact he hadn't been afforded that opportunity, as he had been born and raised in Norway!

Well, I felt for the guy. I told him I had a long history with failure and that I would be happy to help in any way I could. Tears followed and he just left the restaurant without finishing his meal.

That was the last time I ever saw Ben. I hoped that he would one day find his way again.

*　　　　*　　　　*

When I reflect back upon my life, much more than my career, it was my becoming a parent that would define me. Being a father is the hardest, and yet the most fulfilling venture a man can undertake. Part of what makes it so difficult is struggling to balance the responsibilities of being a good man in your own right, with the enthusiasm and excitement of guiding your children while you are still being caught-up in the fun of it all. Add to that the responsibilities of being a good husband, and it can be a daunting task.

The conflicts in balancing all of that can indeed be challenging. Are the choices that you are making best for the life-long success of your child, or are they based on some vicarious drive to fulfill something within yourself? The lines of distinction can be easily crossed. How much do you motivate versus push, or do you just plain let go? How much participation in their undertakings becomes excessive as opposed to supportive? How much do your dreams affect their own developing dreams? Not easy things to sort out, yet the choices we make have monumental impact on our children.

So, being a dad was my number one priority, even if at times, like my Dad before me, I stumbled along that path. My kids are now grown and successful in their own right. That brings me great comfort. So yes, it *Is* the Hard That Makes it Great!

Well, thanks for strolling down memory lane with me. I hope you found the journey as enjoyable to read it was for me to write it. As I said in the beginning, being part of this Game at any level is very special. Somehow, it just has a unique way of staying with you; now *fifty* years and counting for me.

My Year, 1965 was a blessed time in so many ways. To me, it was when the Grain of Life *and* the wonderful Game of Baseball Ran True.

Moose and Bob, Nearly Fifty Years Later.

ACKNOWLEDGEMENTS AND CREDITS

First and foremost I would like to express my deepest appreciation to the Chicago White Sox and to the Chicago Daily News. What an experience you provided to all of us Bat Boys over the years.

Special thanks go to my Visiting Team Crew, Pat (Luke) Ivers and Gregory Driskell and to the Home town kids across the Diamond; Fred Croft, Tom Brzezinski and George Sims. Wherever you all might be today, thanks for all the memories. And, to Sharkey. You taught us a lot. May you always rest in peace, Sir!

Now, for my last story: Many months ago, just when I thought I was finished with writing the book, I gave that draft to a baseball buddy, Mike Trautner. (By the way, his college-age kid Alex, is an ambidextrous pitcher... the first I have seen live and he his darn good, throwing naturally both as a righty and a lefty... cool.) Mike is not one just to pay compliments when asked for his opinion. After a while I heard back from him.

He said it was OK, but that it could be bigger and more expansive, actually more like "a real book" I think he hinted. So I went back to the drawing board. I dug deep and I was able to generate a whole bunch of additional interesting content. After all, it's not easy to remember *everything* that happened fifty years ago! But I made some progress.

With that draft nearly finished, I sent it to my friend Adam Rochon who has great editing skills. He loved it, but he wanted to hear more about what happened to Bob and the White Sox in *My Year*.

Well, I wrote on and sent that draft back to him and Mike. This time, I guess Mike decided that he would lead by example and he began sending me some of his ideas. The net result is the work you see before you today. Without the help of those two guys, this book would probably have remained just a long forgotten family heirloom.

Thanks and appreciation do not do justice to their contributions to When the Grain Ran True. But in the end, that's all these two highly talented, but equally humble friends would accept. I guess that means that they will be receiving autographed copies!

From when I first started writing this book, one person has encouraged me and provided guidance tirelessly... my brother Larry. And through each iteration and version, he was there to read each one, catching many typos with his "eagle-eye" and to cheer me on. Just like he did in My Year!

My Brother Larry. A Pretty Good Editor
and an Even Better Golfer... for a Geezer!

I would also like to express deep appreciation to the following individuals who also contributed greatly to my work: Chris Davis, Ashley Davis, Louann Jensen, Heidi Hough, Bee Hylinski, Ron Kane, Cheryl Davis and Jim Ball. And special thanks to my Aunt Gertie and Uncle Bob for always being there for me.

And of course, my loving bride, Merci. She doesn't know much about baseball, but she knows everything about me! Thanks Sweetie.

My beautiful wife Merci, the Grain Runs the Truest in Her!

In preparing this Memoir, in addition to the credits mentioned along the way, I relied upon images, facts and some descriptions that I retrieved online from:

Major League Baseball.com and Baseball-Reference.com
The Chicago White Sox Website and Related Archives
Sports Illustrated
Wikipedia and Their Acknowledged Sources
The Oakland A's and San Francisco Giants Websites
Baseball Almanac.com
Columbia Pictures
Paramount Pictures
lougehrig.com
The Chicago Public Library Website
The Society for Baseball Research
The Economic History of MLB Baseball

Other Sources include: Comcast Sports Net, Topps Trading Cards, ThisGrandGame.com.

PHOTO GALLERY

Bill Skowron, Bob, Pete Ward and Fred on Our Way
to New York to Start Our Nine Game Road Trip.

That excursion was a blast for Fred and me, but a disaster for the Sox who went just 2W-7L. Moose signed this photo nearly fifty years later!

Bill "Moose" Skowron, Number 57, (Second Row)
was Always Ready to Play Ball!

Even though Weber Catholic High School of Chicago (Class of 1948) did not offer baseball as a sport when he attended, Moose Skowron did play both basketball and football while there. At Purdue University, although on a football scholarship, he hit .500 in his sophomore season for their Baseball Team which led to his 14-year Major League Baseball career.

Newspaper clipping from the Chicago Daily News, April 12, 1965.

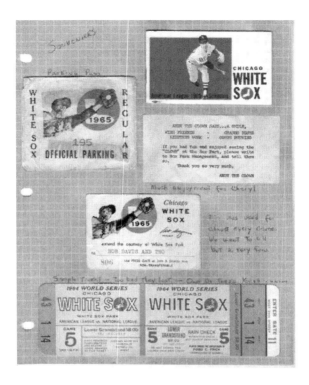

Some treasured White Sox memorabilia saved by my Mom. Included are: 1965 White Sox Pocket Schedule, 1965 Official White Sox Season Entrance and Parking Passes, a "Andy the Clown" Promotional Card... great fun and entertainment for my sister! Lastly, a Printed Game 5 but unused 1964 White Sox World Series Ticket, because the New York Yankees won the American League Pennant that year by just one game. Comment read... "Too bad they (the Sox) lost- One of these years." It would take until 2005 before that dream came true. I got to attend one of those games!

Another Day at the Park!

A Rock N' Roll Band Entertains the Pre-Game Crowd.

*More Than Major Leaguers Played at Comiskey in 1965. The Fab Four
Wanted to Play There Too!*

Ticket Prices for the Concert Were $2.50, $4.50 and $5.50… Such a Deal!

*Pristine Ticket from the Beatles' 1965 Concert at The Park. Then, $2.50.
Now, $700 on EBay!*

My Mom and Dad. Sure Would be Nice to Have One More Catch.

My Son Chris Pitching at Cooperstown Dreams Park.

*Chris and Me (Rear-Center) on One
of His Travel Teams When We Lived in Maryland.*

*Newspaper clippings from when my son, then an incoming high school junior,
pitched a two hit shut-out against the favored cross-town rival, moving Hinsdale
Central into the Summer State High School Tournament. In his senior year, he
lead the pitching staff with a 10-2 record, and a 2.72 ERA, while hitting .440
with 4 home runs, including one grand slam.*

Chris would go on to play in college at Illinois Wesleyan University and after in a men's hardball league where he excelled and had a blast doing so! More importantly though, he would graduate Summa Cum Laude in just 3.5 years. He is now a successful executive with Federated Investors and is married to his lovely and talented wife, Lauren. They reside in Minneapolis, Minnesota where I fear he might be becoming a Twins fan!

*Chris (then eighteen years old) at the "Cell"
on White Sox Prospect Day in 2003.*

The stadium the White Sox built in 1991 for $168 million dollars has since benefited from major renovation projects in the previous decade worth nearly the initial construction cost of the stadium. Originally named "new" Comiskey Park it was to be later renamed U.S. Cellular Field in 2003 for $68 million dollars of valued naming rights stretching over twenty years. This, the same season that the White Sox would host the All-Star game, and unbeknownst to everyone, two years before the White Sox would claim the 2005 World Series crown. The "new" stadium sits upon the former parking lot of "old" Comiskey Park, where in 1965 my Mom and Dad would park our 1961 Buick Skylark right next to Fred's Beatle!

And the Best for Last… My Daughter Ashley Got Her Licks in Too!

Ashley graduated from Hope College in Holland, MI. She was an honor roll student and a very active member of the Sigma Sigma Sorority. She worked as a social worker assisting victims of crime through the court system for several years and is now an Associate Financial Representative with Northwestern Mutual. She and her husband Jose, a Chicago Police Officer, reside in that wonderful city that I still call home… Sweet Home Chicago!

APPENDIX

BAT BOY CONTEST

OFFICIAL RULES

1—All boys 12 to 16 years are eligible. Contestants must be 12 on or before March 26, 1966 and may not be 17 until Oct. 31, 1966. The immediate family of an employee of the Newspaper Division of Field Enterprises, Inc. or the Chicago White Sox is not eligible.

2—Each boy may enter only once. An official entry blank which appears in The Daily News or a reasonable facsimile must be used. Entry blanks must be signed by a parent or legal guardian.

3—Contestants need not reside in the Chicago area. However, boys who live outside metropolitan Chicago must provide name, Chicago address and relationship of an adult with whom they will reside if they win.

4—Each entry blank must be accompanied by a statement of 50 or less words, written or printed in your own handwriting on an 8½x11 sheet of white paper, entitled "Why I want to be a White Sox bat boy in 1966."

5—Entries must be mailed to Daily News Bat Boy Contest, P.O. Box 3425, Chicago 60654. Envelopes must be postmarked no later than midnight, Saturday, March 26, 1966, and must reach The Daily News before noon on March 29.

6—Finalists will be selected on the basis of neatness, originality, aptness and clarity of their 50-word statement. Baseball ability is not considered.

7—Fifteen finalists will be chosen and personally interviewed by a panel of judges during a luncheon at White Sox Park April 2. The finalists will be notified on March 31 or April 1 and must be present at the luncheon to be eligible for the top prizes.

8—The White Sox bat boy, visiting team bat boy, assistants, ball boys and camp-prize winners will be selected on the basis of personality, character, attitude, sportsmanship and baseball interest.

9—The Winner, runner-up, assistant and ball boys all become employees of the Chicago White Sox and are subject to the rules, regulations and working conditions of that organization.

OFFICIAL PRIZES

1st PLACE

1—Appointment as official '66 White Sox bat boy. If any conflict arises over school, the White Sox will provide an interim bat boy.

2—A regular salary and use of a White Sox uniform during the season.

3—A $1,000 cash scholarship, to be deposited in trust until the boy is ready to attend college or vocational school.

4—An all-expenses-paid, seven-day road trip with the White Sox from July 4 - 10 to New York, Washington and Boston.

5—Appointment as White Sox bat boy for World Series games in White Sox Park.

6—Free tickets to a regular White Sox home game for the entire student body and faculty of the winning boy's school.

2nd PLACE

1—Appointment as official 1966 visiting bat boy at White Sox Park.

2—A regular salary and use of a uniform during the season.

3—An all-expenses-paid, seven-day road trip with the White Sox (same dates and cities as the winning bat boy).

4—Appointment as visiting team bat boy for World Series games in White Sox Park.

3rd & 4th PLACES

1—Appointments as assistants, respectively, to the White Sox and visiting team bat boys during the 1966 season.

2—A regular salary and use of a uniform during the season.

5th & 6th PLACES

1—Appointments as official ball boys along the left- and right-field foul lines during all White Sox home games.

2—A regular salary and use of a uniform during the season.

7th, 8th, 9th & 10th PLACES

An all-expenses-paid, three-week stay this summer at the White Sox Boys Camp at Brothertown, Wisconsin . . . June 26 to July 16.

PLUS These Prizes . . .

1—In addition to an invitation to the April 2 luncheon at White Sox Park, the 15 finalists will each receive a 1966 White Sox season pass for himself and two guests.

2—The top 35 contestants will each receive a baseball autographed by the entire White Sox team.

3—Every boy who enters the contest will receive two free tickets to the White Sox-Washington Senators doubleheader Sunday, June 5.

The Chicago Daily News Bat Boy Contest Rules and Highlights.

179

1965 Chicago White Sox Roster

Uniform #	Pitchers	Height	Weight	Throws	Bats	DOB
47	Greg Bollo	6-04	183	Right	Right	11/16/43
30	John Buzhardt	6-02	198	Right	Right	08/17/36
28	Eddie Fisher	6-02	200	Right	Right	07/16/36
20	Joe Horlen	6-00	175	Right	Right	08/14/37
19	Bruce Howard	6-02	180	Right	Both	03/23/43
25	Tommy John	6-03	185	Left	Right	05/22/43
17	Frank Lary	5-11	180	Right	Right	04/10/30
23	Bob Locker	6-03	200	Right	Both	03/15/38
43	Gary Peters	6-02	200	Left	Left	04/21/37
32	Juan Pizarro	5-11	190	Left	Left	02/07/37
31	Hoyt Wilhelm	6-00	195	Right	Right	07/26/22
26	Ted Wills	6-02	200	Left	Left	02/09/34
Uniform #	Catchers	Height	Weight	Throws	Bats	DOB
2	Smoky Burgess	5-08	187	Right	Left	02/06/27
46	Duane Josephson	6-00	195	Right	Right	06/03/42
12	J.C. Martin	6-02	200	Right	Left	12/13/36
5	Johnny Romano	5-11	205	Right	Right	08/23/34
18	Jimmie Schaffer	5-09	185	Right	Right	04/05/36
Uniform #	Infielders	Height	Weight	Throws	Bats	DOB
7	Don Buford	5-08	165	Right	Both	02/02/37
18	Gene Freese	5-11	175	Right	Right	01/08/34
4	Ron Hansen	6-03	200	Right	Right	04/05/38
24	Tommy McCraw	6-00	183	Left	Left	11/21/40
14	Bill Skowron	5-11	195	Right	Right	12/18/30
8	Pete Ward	6-01	200	Right	Left	07/26/37
6	Al Weis	6-00	170	Right	Both	04/02/38
Uniform #	Outfielders	Height	Weight	Throws	Bats	DOB
1	Tommie Agee	5-11	195	Right	Right	08/09/42
16	Ken Berry	5-11	180	Right	Right	05/10/41
9	Danny Cater	5-11	180	Right	Right	02/25/40
44	Jim Hicks	6-03	205	Right	Right	05/18/40
11	Dave Nicholson	6-02	215	Right	Right	08/29/39
3	Floyd Robinson	5-09	175	Right	Left	05/09/36
40	Bill Voss	6-02	160	Left	Left	10/31/43
Uniform #	Utility	Height	Weight	Throws	Bats	DOB
34	Bill Heath	5-08	175	Right	Left	03/10/39
26	Dick Kenworthy	5-09	170	Right	Right	04/01/41
29	Marv Staehle	5-10	172	Right	Left	03/13/42

Uniform #	Field Coaches	Height	Weight	Throws	Bats	DOB
10	Al Lopez, *Manager*	5-11	165	Right	Right	08/08/08
37	Ray Berres	5-09	170	Right	Right	08/31/07
33	Tony Cuccinello	5-07	160	Right	Right	11/08/07
39	Don Gutteridge	5-10	165	Right	Right	06/18/12
36	Charlie Metro	5-11	178	Right	Right	04/28/18

A BASEBALL FAN'S RETROSPECTIVE ON THE 1965 WHITE SOX SEASON

*Compiled by Mike Trautner with Contributions
From Glenn Davis and Adam Rochon*

The 1965 baseball season opened for the American League as usual with banner excitement as teams maneuvered to strengthen their teams. Among the big name off-season transactions that year, the New York Yankees traded starting pitcher Ralph Terry to the Cleveland Indians, the Los Angeles Dodgers had dealt home run slugger Frank Howard to the Washington Senators for quality pitching which included Claude Osteen, and Cleveland once again acquired slugger Rocky Colavito from the Kansas City Athletics.

During the off-season, the Chicago White Sox had bolstered their catching position through a complex three-way trade involving the Indians and the Athletics. The net result was that the White Sox would be reunited with a now All-Star catcher in Johnny Romano while obtaining a promising young left-handed pitcher in Tommy John. They also acquired another budding star in Tommie Agee.

While there was always some degree of off-season trade activity between the clubs in those days, big name franchise player trades were still somewhat uncommon. Free agency was not yet in place for the ball players, so the trades were much frequent than by today's standards.

With regards to the White Sox off-season trades, they had a definite need to specifically address and upgrade their catcher position from an offensive production standpoint. Although current White Sox catcher J.C. Martin was an acceptably good catcher, in 1964 he had hit an anemic .197 batting average with just 4 home runs, contributing just 22 RBI's to the team.

On the other hand, Johnny Romano their newly reunited off-season acquisition was now a proven two-time All-Star catcher, hitting .241 in 1964 for the Indians with 19 home runs and 47 RBI's while playing in just 106 games. Catcher J.C. Martin was retained as the team's specialist for their knuckleball pitchers, Eddie Fisher, and especially for treacherous flutterball thrower Hoyt Wilhelm, both picked up a couple years beforehand.

The White Sox began their 1965 regular season with a slight sputter. However, by the tenth game of the season, the Sox had defeated the Washington Senators at Comiskey Park and found themselves in an American League tie with the Minnesota Twins.

Over the next thirty games, the White Sox would remain in first place after twenty-five such contests, slipping into a half-game second place standing only four times during this stretch.

The month of May was certainly fortuitous for the White Sox. By May 18th, they expanded their League lead over the Minnesota Twins to 4-1/2 games after Eddie Fisher's 5-4 save over the Athletics. Although Fisher would not start a single game during the entire season, the right-handed knuckleball relief pitcher would eventually post a 15-7 record, a 2.40 ERA and a remarkable 24 game save credit which earned him a trip to the 1965 All-Star game.

The month of June was a battle for the Southsider's. The Sox finished the month, 1-1/2 games out of first place. The boys had fought hard during the month, never falling more than three games behind the Twins, and actually sharing the League lead with them on one date. Still, the grind began.

Behind the scenes, challenges were nevertheless brewing. Although June had been a somewhat respectable 15W-13L month, it could have and should have gone better.

Both "Pistol" Pete Ward and Bill "Moose" Skowron were physically ailing with injury. One Friday night game, in early June while at Yankee Stadium, Pete Ward pulled himself out of a scoreless extra-inning game. While that action may have appeared rather innocuous to many casual fans, Pete would go on to miss twenty-four games that season, many of them during the months of June and July.

Meanwhile, Moose Skowron was as well ailing with a rib and back injury which began impacting his game in mid-June as well. Late inning defensive replacements for Moose also began in earnest starting on June 23rd against the Senators and increased in frequency as the All-Star break approached.

Ultimately, on July 9th he was removed from the White Sox line-up and would go on to miss seven consecutive games, in addition to the esteemed All-Star game. Such a shame as he had been selected to start first base for the American League at that summer classic at Metropolitan Stadium in Bloomington, MN.

As the season progressed, it became increasingly apparent that the freakish automobile accident that Ward had suffered after attending a Chicago Blackhawk's hockey game at the start of the baseball season was much more serious than he initially believed. Pete would continue to have recurring neck spasms throughout the 1965 season which undoubtedly affected his play.

Despite the nagging injury, Pete was chosen for the cover shot of the June 7, 1965 issue of Sports Illustrated. Unfortunately for Ward and the White Sox, a young upshot Heavyweight Prize Fighter named Muhammad Ali had knocked-out Sonny Liston in the first round of a most controversial fight on May 25th in Lewiston, Maine.

That surprising outcome trumped the newsworthiness of the Ward cover and it was replaced with one of the Champ... perhaps the greatest Heavyweight in boxing history. In any case he sure thought so, proclaiming that "I am the greatest" throughout much of his career. His work in the ring seemed to confirm that sentiment to many fans and critics alike.

As for Pete's SI cover, the artwork was eventually gifted to him, but it never hit the newsstands. That one moment in Maine changed that outcome forever.

The Sports Illustrated Cover that Got KO'd by Muhammad Ali!

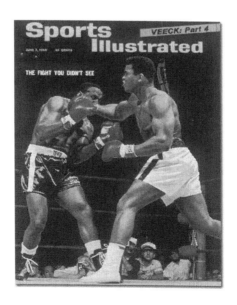

Perhaps the Greatest Heavyweight Boxer Ever, Muhammad Ali KO's Sonny Liston in the 1ˢᵗ Round.

The following season Pete suffered from increased back pain which reduced his playing time to just eighty-four games, an injury that would hamper and eventually curtail his playing career. Years later he wrote in a news article that he had, "No regrets about the great Sox career that wasn't." He, like Moose Skowron, would never blame an injury for lowered performance on the ball field.

Despite the unexpected adversity that the White Sox were experiencing from two of their top hitters, the team managed to keep afloat in July with a 12W-16L record. However the Twins, behind the power hitting of Harmon Killebrew (25 HR), Bob Allison (23 HR), Don Mincher (22 HR), Jimmie Hall (20 HR), Zoilo Versalles (19 HR) and Tony Oliva (16 HR and .321 BA) began to heat up, rattling off a nine-game winning streak just before the All-Star break. That left them finishing the month of July with an impressive record of 22W-9L.

Meanwhile, the White Sox quickly found themselves 9-1/2 games behind first place at the conclusion of July. A particularly painful nine day, three city road trip to New York, Detroit, and Cleveland, the Sox went 2W-7L, certainly contributing heavily to those dismal July results.

The merciless month of July for the White Sox was however fortunately broken up for a few days by the 1965 All-Star game. The former Washington Senators had moved to Metropolitan Stadium in 1961 and became the Minnesota Twins, home of the 1965 All-Star game.

White Sox Manager Al Lopez headed up the American League squad in the newly renovated Metropolitan Stadium in Bloomington, MN. Interestingly, two Second Place League Managers, not the generally appointed Pennant-winning World Series Managers from the previous season, were designated to manage the 1965 All-Star team.

As it happened, the defeated 1964 World Series Manager Yogi Berra of the New York Yankees was surprisingly fired by Yankee ball player turned Manager, and now General Manager Ralph Houk. Mr. Berra thus departed the Bronx Bombers and took a player/coach position with the recently expanded National League team, the New York Mets, in neighboring Queens, where he remained for eight seasons.

As that played out, the opposing and winning World Series Manager Johnny Keane, skipper of the St. Louis Cardinals, subsequently left his National League Pennant-winning team to fill the now emptied helm of the New York Yankees. Famed Cardinal left-fielder Red Schoendienst would backfill his position and go on to manage the St. Louis Cardinals for the next twelve years. Johnny Keane on the other hand would unfortunately last only twenty games into his second season before being fired as the Yankee Manager.

The significance of these two off-season manager movements consequently altered the usual structured composition of the 1965 All-Star Game as both World Series Managers had switched professional leagues. For the first time in history, the two skippers managing the All-Star Game would both be representatives of Second Place Teams, NL Manager Gene Mauch of the Philadelphia Phillies, and AL Manager Al Lopez of the Chicago White Sox.

The Newly Renovated Home of the Minnesota Twins and of the 1965 All-Star Game.

Unlike today, the 1965 All-Star players were chosen solely by the Major League managers, coaches, and players, and not by the fans. Back in 1957, Cincinnati fans had stuffed the All-Star ballot box, selecting 8 of 9 National League All-Star starters as… you guessed it… Cincinnati Redleg players. Commissioner Ford Frick had to step in to alleviate the injustice by naming Willie Mays and Hank Aaron as starters to the outfield, while furthermore preventing fans from voting in future All-Star player selections.

In any event, as mentioned, the Chicago White Sox had two players selected to the 1965 All-Star team, Eddie Fisher and Starting first baseman Moose Skowron (.275 BA, 11 HR at All-Star break). However, due to his nagging rib injury, Moose was in temporary dry-dock and could not play.

To fill that vacancy, Al Lopez selected Joe Pepitone of the New York Yankees to the All-Star roster (.262 BA, 9 HR at All-Star break). However it was "Killer" Harmon Killebrew of the Minnesota Twins (.271 BA, 16 HR at All-Star-break), the first player to ever be elected to three different All-Star positions, who played the entire All-Star Game at first base on his home field.

Joe Pepitone, a natural first baseman, now a two-time All-Star, sat on the bench the entire game until the last out of the game approached. He was then called to pinch hit for Sox pitcher Eddie Fisher, with the tying run on second base and flame thrower Bob Gibson on the mound. Pepitone worked the count to 3-2, before striking out swinging to end the game. Even many American League fans were happy to see the somewhat brash and always flamboyant Pepitone fail to reach base. In the end the final score was 6-5, the National League winning the annual exhibition contest.

Albeit, it was a strange All-Star game. Not only did two Second Place Managers lead the All-Star contest for the first time in history, but even more remarkably, for the first time in All-Star history (dating back to July 6, 1933 at Comiskey Park) there was not a single New York Yankee player in the starting line-up. In fact, the only repeating American League starter from the previous year was third baseman, Brooks Robinson. Amazing!

Following the All-Star break and their dismal July results, the White Sox managed to turn the ship around and began firing on all eight cylinders once again. They enjoyed an extremely respectable August, going 22W-12L which included a ten-game winning streak during the month. Monthly scoring production was at its highest at 129 runs and was spread fairly evenly throughout the line-up with seven players posting ten or more RBI's; Romano (18), Robinson (17), Skowron (16), Buford (13), Carter (12), Ward (12), and Hansen (10). However, the Twins had an August that nearly matched the White Sox at 19W-13L, so the net gain for them at the end of the month was just a two game improvement, now trailing 7-1/2 games behind the Twins. But the Southsider's battled on.

By Monday, September 6th, after a doubleheader sweep against the Los Angeles Angels at Comiskey Park, the White Sox were now just 4-1/2 games back of Minnesota, with the Twins scheduled to visit Comiskey for a final two-game set beginning on Wednesday after the White Sox made-up a rain date with the Indians on Tuesday. The Southsider's collective team fan base was ecstatic. If the Sox could get past the Indians, they could meet up with the Twins trailing by just four games for the two set finale with 19 games still remaining to close out the season. However, sadly and abruptly, it was just not to be as Cleveland won the make-up game, and the Twins swept the two game set, leaving the White Sox seven games out of first place.

What a swing of events, and what an immense let down! The bubble had burst, and it now appeared that it was just a matter of time before the White Sox would become mathematically eliminated from contention.

That day would come on Sunday, September 26th, although the White Sox would be in the midst of a five- game win streak, finishing off the Yankees in a three-game series on the road. Meanwhile, twenty-five-year-old left-handed Minnesota Twin pitcher Jim Kaat would valiantly pitch an impressive complete game. Carefully spreading eight hits and ten strikeouts over nine innings against his former team, the Washington Senators, in a rather tense 2-1 victory at D.C. Stadium. The Twins had officially clinched the 1965 American League pennant.

The White Sox did not fold at season end though, winning 12 of their last 15 games. The Sox finished proudly at 95-67, in second place, twenty-eight games above a .500 winning percentage, but sadly for Chicago, seven full games out of first place. The bottom of the ninth had come to the Sox season, but they went out swinging!

Most baseball fans going into the 1965 World Series thought that the depth of Minnesota Twins' power hitting coupled with their superb pitching would easily overtake the Los Angeles Dodgers, who had slightly below average hitting, but extraordinary pitching.

1965 Regular Season Statistics

	RBI's	Runs per game	Home Runs	ERA
Los Angeles	548	3.75	78	2.81
Minnesota	711	4.78	150	3.14

After the completion of the second game of the 1965 World Series, everyone's initial convictions seemed confirmed. The Minnesota Twins would dominate the Los Angeles Dodgers in the early part of the series.

The Twins had taken the first two games, behind the pitching of Mudcat Grant and Jim Kaat, defeating the Dodger's top pitching aces, Koufax and Drysdale. Minnesota had outscored Los Angeles by a combined ten runs over the first two games 13-3.

Enter, Claude Osteen, the pitcher that the Los Angeles Dodgers had obtained from the Washington Senators during the off-season, relinquishing their big slugger Frank Howard to consummate the trade. Osteen had gone 15-15 during the regular season, but he held a Top 10 National League leading 2.79 ERA. In the biggest game of his pitching career, with the Dodgers down 0-2 in the series, Claude Osteen, pitched the game of his life, a complete game 4-0 shutout, against Cuban-born Minnesota Twin Camilo Pascual.

That Game 3 victory was the lightning bolt lift of energy that the Dodgers were looking for and needed to turn the series around. In Game 4, Don Drysdale beat Mudcat Grant, in a 7-2 complete game, tossing 11 strikeouts. His only two mistakes were surrendering two solo shot home runs, one to Harmon Killibrew and the other to Tony Oliva.

In Game 5, Sandy Koufax responded by throwing a complete game shutout against Jim Kaat, 7-0. Koufax got all the run support he would need in the first inning as the Dodgers scored two runs. Shortstop Maury Wills led the first inning off with a ground rule double to deep right field. The second batter, third baseman Jim Gilliam singled to right centerfield, and the speedy Maury Wills easily scored from second base. Centerfielder Willie Davis then laid a bunt down the third base line. The catch at first base was misplayed by the covering second baseman, allowing Gilliam to score, and Davis to make it all the way to third base on the play. The Dodgers would not need any more run support, but they plated an additional five runs throughout the completion of the game.

Meanwhile, Koufax fanned ten Twins, walking only one. The momentum of the series had now shifted to the Dodgers who had won three straight games after dropping the first two games in somewhat humiliating fashion.

Game 6 was played in Minnesota, Claude Osteen was the Dodger pitcher and he opposed Twins ace Mudcat Grant (21-7 regular season). This time Mudcat who was now 1-1 in the series, pitching on two days rest, beat the Dodgers with his arm and his bat. In the bottom of the sixth inning, with Osteen out of the game, Mudcat hit a three run blast to deep left centerfield off of relief pitcher Howie Reed final score, 5-1. The series was now tied 3-3.

Game 7, the marquee match-up in the series finale, Koufax versus Kaat. Both pitchers were 1-1 in the series going into the deciding game. Both Koufax and Kaat were pitching on two days rest, in a pitching rematch of Game 5.

In the earlier match-up Koufax threw a gem, a complete game shutout with ten strikeouts. In the series finale, Koufax duplicated his earlier performance, again throwing a complete game shutout and again with ten strikeouts. Over his last two combined games of the 1965 World Series, eighteen innings of high-level tense competition, Koufax yielded just seven hits, bolstered by twenty strikeouts, while surrendering not one run to the opposition. The Los Angeles Dodgers were 1965 World Champions with Sandy Koufax of course selected MVP of the Series!

In amazing retrospect, three of the four World Series games won that year by the Dodgers were exacted on complete game shutout pitching performances (Koufax 2, Osteen 1). The other winning performance belonged to Don Drysdale in Game 4, who pitched a complete five hit, two run, eleven strikeout game. Over the course of those *four complete game* winning performances in the series, over thirty six innings against the power hitting Minnesota Twins, the combined winning Dodger pitching staff (Koufax 2, Drysdale 1, and Osteen 1) collected thirty-three strikeouts, surrendering just seventeen hits, while yielding just two total runs.

In 1965, it appeared that the old baseball adage, "Good pitching will beat good hitting," had come true before our very eyes.

It would take more than twenty years before Minnesota recaptured that flag.

1965 White Sox Promo Piece, No Expense Spared.
Yup, that's genuine Mimeograph folks! I can still smell the vinegary stench that
spirits-based ink made... Yuk!

Made in the USA
Las Vegas, NV
10 October 2021